High Style

High Style

RON WOODSON AND JAIME RUMMERFIELD

FOREWORD BY SARA RUFFIN COSTELLO

PHOTOGRAPHS BY JONATHAN SHAPIRO

CHRONICLE BOOKS
SAN FRANCISCO

Dedicated to Tom and Dana.

Page 253 constitutes a continuation of this copyright page.

Library of Congress Cataloging-in-Publication
Data available.

ISBN : 978-0-8118-6141-0

Manufactured in China.

Book Design/Creative Direction by Jon Ritt of Pool
Book Design by Jon Ritt, Tony Jagoda, Brian Toth
Cover Design by Jay Peter Salvas

10 9 8 7 6 5 4 3 2 1

Chronicle Books LLC
680 Second Street
San Francisco, California 94107

www.chroniclebooks.com

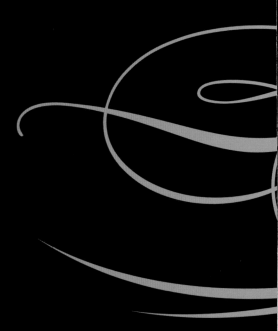

Table Of Contents

CHAPTER		
	FOREWORD BY SARA RUFFIN COSTELLO	6
	INTRODUCTION	8
1	MAKING IT WORK	32
2	I LOVE L.A.	60
3	HOLLYWOOD STYLE	122
4	MINING FOR GOLD	144
5	CALIFORNIA DREAMIN'	182
6	LIVING IN THE MOMENT	214
	AFTERWORD	249
	ACKNOWLEDGMENTS	252
	RESOURCES	253
	ADDITIONAL CREDITS	253
	INDEX	254

FOREWORD

High Style is the missing book in your design library. It dutifully honors the tenets of good decorating: beauty, proportion, comfort, and surprise—lots of surprise! Woodson and Rummerfield create cinematically narrative environments that advocate the pursuit of gin and tonics. These are houses that make you want to throw open the front doors and entertain. Living rooms are wrapped in bold color and pattern, tempered with geometry, and playfully winking at scale; bedrooms are cocoons of glamour boasting tufted velvet wing chairs, custom upholstered leather beds, and miles of silk on crisp white sheets. The hallmark of their design is joyful exuberance. The overall aesthetic is punk-rock prep. Woodson and Rummerfield's philosophy? The pursuit of pleasure, taken very seriously.

—Sara Ruffin Costello, Creative Director, *Domino* magazine

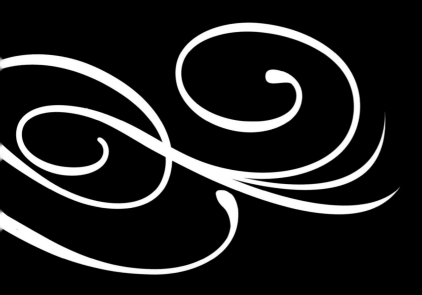

Introduction

We believe the world is a beautiful place;

we like it this way. After over twenty years' combined experience as interior designers, we've seen firsthand that everyone can benefit from an extra dose of beauty in their daily lives. If you're reading this book, then you just may want what we want: to surround yourself with fun, glamour, and lushness—and, above all, to enjoy the pleasure that beauty brings.

When it comes to decorating, beauty doesn't belong to a single time or place. Beauty is not buying all your furniture from one retailer or paying top dollar. Beauty is a unique mix of objects from around the world, from the past and present, family heirlooms and mass market finds that reflect you, your life, and your interests. We find beauty in the most unexpected places and find joy in sharing it with others, and we've dedicated our life's work to showcasing the wonderment in living well.

Our approach to design is a whole-life sensibility—it's finding that special, conversation-starting piece and knowing just where to put it; it's breaking out the crystal and china every day, not just for holiday dinners or special occasions; it's scouring antique stores, flea markets, and your grandmother's attic for items just waiting for a fresh new look that screams of your personality; and it's making a fabulous outfit or tabletop look perfect in any situation. We capture this look and feel in our Los Angeles retail shop, where you'll find our furniture and fabric collections. And the look permeates our designs for clients, which combine California modern with vintage Hollywood decadence. We call our brand of mixing the old with the new, the modern and vintage, "Modage."

opposite
Jaime and Ron in the Woodson & Rummerfield's showroom.

California—Los Angeles in particular—has long been celebrated for its laid-back-yet-luxurious lifestyle. We have been heavily influenced by L.A.'s heyday of cocktail parties and grand hotel gatherings, but we live in the modern world of sleek, clean lines and simple opulence. The Modage sensibility arises from our desire to take our clients back to a time when high living was an art form in itself, without sacrificing the sophisticated contributions of modern stylists. Modage is our signature brand of high style; it says, "Life is the occasion. Enjoy it. Celebrate it." Surrounding yourself with glamour, fun, and outrageous comfort is only the first step on a magic carpet ride to living the good life.

opposite

A wonderful mix of old and new objects, including a rare painting by textiles designer Florence Broadhurst. Here antique Staffordshire dogs complement modern pillar candlestick holders made of resin.

below

This Florence Broadhurst installation in our showroom is just one example of the beautiful spaces we create by mixing the old and new. Our inspiration comes from everyday objects and images, such as peacock feathers, indigenous plant life, the city of Los Angeles, and vintage forms.

following pages

Ron and Jaime out on the town at The Dresden Room. Old supper clubs like the Dresden offer a glimpse into the Golden Age of Hollywood.

As a Los Angeles design duo, we are freshly inspired every day by our surroundings, from Old Hollywood and Spanish-style buildings to ultramodern architecture in some of the city's toniest neighborhoods. We are uplifted by the changing colors of the ocean and by L.A.'s bright parade of patterns, lights, oversized billboards, and painted signs, by the details we see on brick facades, stores' international selection of cutting-edge fashions, and by the many cultures alive in the city. We combine these influences with the surreal world of Hollywood celebrity, fantastic soirées, and chic events. This is our everyday life. Angelenos have access to a huge variety of elements with which to create their own personal styles, and so they have become creative and inventive risk-takers, always ready to explore and always willing to push the envelope. That's why, for us, Los Angeles is the epitome of high style.

below

Los Angeles has its own unique personality, which influences us in so many ways; from the coast to downtown, the city speaks to us with a vibrant visual language.

opposite, top

The skyline of downtown Los Angeles sparkles with magic on summer nights.

opposite, bottom

While we enjoy a treat from an ice-cream street cart in Silver Lake, a wall of bold graffiti inspires us to create energetic color palettes.

14

DO
COME
IN

WWW.WANDRDESIGN.COM

THE HOUSE OF DESIGN

We built our boutique shop, Woodson & Rummerfield's House of Design, to reflect our unique style. In fact, the shop is set up to look just like a home, and a fabulous one at that. Unlike some showrooms, which are big open spaces, our shop is compartmentalized into fully furnished, inviting rooms, like a real home. When you walk in the door, you'll see we have a living room, dining room, bar, and more. There's even a quaint little garden out front to welcome visitors.

When we opened in 2005, we had no idea what type of destination the shop would become. We wanted a place to showcase our treasures, but we figured it would serve primarily as the perfect setting for us to try out ideas for our clients. Word got out, though, and our shop is now a hub of designer sourcing for famous decorators, celebrities, hipsters, and those of discerning taste from all walks of life. We've had people like Cameron Diaz and Beck drop by for something special. Designers to the stars like Jonathan Adler, Nate Berkus, Kenneth Brown, and Martyn Lawrence Bullard shop W&R for perfect pieces to outfit their clients' homes. The shop is Los Angeles at its finest—surprising, chic, and friendly. All kinds of shoppers come to us for our "eye," and we do not disappoint. We set the stage and welcome people right off the street to partake in the design experience.

Our building on La Cienega Boulevard was built in 1939. In the 1930s, '40s, and '50s, the boulevard was home to many vaudevillian, silent film, and, later, "talkie" theaters. Home to some of Tinseltown's first movie premieres, La Cienega was the cat's meow. Rumor has it that many buildings on the strip were used by Hollywood studios as rehearsal spaces. Our building is known to be a former dance studio, and later home to the Court Theater, which featured live stage performances. We can just picture Judy Garland in her tap shoes dancing along our floors; the storefront still carries that Old Hollywood charm today.

When designing our shop, we took many cues from the original architecture. The bay windows still flank double glass doors, with decorative stone urns on either side to greet you. An intimate second level became the perfect location for our design studio and library. We were thrilled to find a beautifully painted, Art Deco–style floor in one of the rooms, and though we later discovered it was not original (it was done in the 1980s), we kept it. The former theater's high ceilings are perfect for our living room installations. We put a faux fireplace and antique mantel where there was once a window that opened onto a cinder-block wall, which we share with our hot spot restaurant neighbor, Koi. The storefront space was occupied by a beauty salon for over two decades before being abandoned for years, so you can imagine the state of disrepair we found it in. We cleaned it up, polished, painted, and brought it back to life. In six months, we were up and running.

Shopping at the House of Design provides inspiration and materials for visitors, but it also serves as a great introduction to who we are. Our design aesthetic and personalities are showcased in each room, just as are our objets d'art.

previous pages
Woodson & Rummerfield's House of Design storefront in West Hollywood invites shoppers to enter and delight in the Modage experience.

opposite
This dining room installation in our showroom exemplifies how simple it can be to create a glamorous, comfortable room using one key accent color. Punches of green throughout create interest against the traditional black-and-white palette. We also love the contrast in textures between the smooth, modern Lucite and plush green velvet of these 1970s chairs. Solid-black painted walls and black-and-white striped wallpaper interact harmoniously with the scaled patterns also found in the room.

following pages
Woodson & Rummerfield's living room installation, featuring furnishings from the Versace Home Collection mixed with one of a kind objets d'art, decorative products from Vellum, and our Chrysanthemum wallpaper.

below, clockwise from top

An iconic La Cienega street sign at Sunset Boulevard. We are always thrilled when our fellow design collaborators come by to shop at our boutique. Here we are with Sami Hayek (top right), Dean McDermott and Tori Spelling at Woodson & Rummerfield's House of Design" (bottom right), Aussie David Lennie, owner of Signature prints, pops in the showroom for a visit (bottom left).

opposite

We love to stroll through the neighborhood that surrounds Woodson & Rummerfield's House of Design. We always find something that brings us joy.

WHY WE DO WHAT WE DO: RON WOODSON

I was born when the Rat Pack were at the peak of their careers, and jazz was cool, baby. I'm the product of two second-generation Angelenos; my parents were part of the black bourgeoisie and arts scene of the 1950s, '60s, and '70s. My father was a jazz musician who worked with many of the greats, such as Lena Horne, Ella Fitzgerald, Sammy Davis Jr., and Bobby Short, to name just a few. His sextet frequently played parties at tobacco and energy heiress Doris Duke's home, Falcon Lair. I was exposed to a lot of amazing people and places that most other children my age were not. Doris Duke actually bought me my first Christian Dior suit—how could I not develop a fashion bug? I still love the feel of a well-made suit.

From an early age, I possessed a keen sense of style. When I was eight years old, my parents bought me a very fancy faux-fur-and-leather winter coat for special occasions. That same year, I went on a camping trip to Big Bear Lake, California. I decided to wear the coat on my camping trip, but not before my father pulled me aside to ask if I was sure I should wear my nice coat to go camping, and to ask how I would feel if I got the coat dirty or ruined it altogether. I thought it was a perfect time to wear the coat—I assured him I wouldn't ruin it "because I'm not going to get dirty," and I didn't.

The rich heritage of my family gave me an appreciation for all things beautiful, and it gave me the material for developing a creative spirit very early in life. When I was 10 years old, I attended art classes every Saturday morning at the Los Angeles County Museum of Art. All week long, I looked forward to Saturday and the new pieces of art I would create. My parents wanted me to follow in my father's footsteps, but a career in music didn't speak to me the way working with other art forms did, so I chose another direction. I actually received my first college degree in finance because I like to use both the left and right sides of my brain, and I wanted to broaden my business skills. Unfortunately, business as a discipline just is not in my DNA, so I went back to school,

this time attending UCLA's Architecture and Interior Design program.

I began my professional design career as an art consultant and custom framer—art in all its mediums has always been a key element in my design work. I also love to combine my passion for travel with my collector's eye to acquire beautiful pieces of art and furnishings from around the world.

Jaime and I met through mutual friends who had known us both for several years and insisted that we get together. I held a dinner party; you're always nervous when another designer comes to your house, and I was worried when I noticed Jaime looking around. But we got on really well, finding out that we had similar goals and design philosophies. We talked easily about everything from business to our personal lives. Not long after, Jaime threw her own dinner party. This time, I got to look around her place the way she had mine. But now I understood—she owned many of the same vintage items that I loved, pedigree things you don't see every day or everywhere. I had sworn off business partners based on past experiences, but with Jaime it was a completely organic connection. We knew we had a complementary sensibility. Soon, the House of Design was off and running, and we never looked back.

below, left to right

Ron's father, Buddy, playing bass for Sammy Davis Jr., 1958; Ron showing a keen sense of style at a very early age, 1970; Ron's parents, Elgar and Buddy (right), on their wedding night with friends, 1958; Elgar, Grandfather Willie, Grandmother Julia, and Aunt Celestine, 1955.

opposite, top

Ron's grandfather, Frank, founder of the Watts Symphony Orchestra, early 1960s; Ron's sister, Julie, Ron, and Elgar, 1966.

opposite, middle

Elgar, 1961; Ron's grandparents, Frank and Geneva, mid-1940s; Ron's aunts, Genevieve and Dorothy, 1954; Ron's father playing bass at a Los Angeles supper club, early 1950s.

opposite, bottom

Ron (right) and friend Sebastian (left) going on a camping trip to Big Bear Lake in California; Elgar (right), Duke Ellington (middle), and Elgar's friend Sarah (left).

WHY WE DO WHAT WE DO: JAIME RUMMERFIELD

I was born in the LBC (Long Beach, California) in the 1970s. My parents were beachy hippies, so my childhood was one long summer of love. They encouraged and inspired me to explore my creativity and follow my bliss. They even got me a green plastic desk that looked like a little drafting table, where I would happily draw and read for hours on end.

My grandparents inspired me, too, but their style was entirely different from my parents'. My dad's father, Grandpa Salvatore, was a very talented furniture craftsman from Boiano, Italy, who instilled in me an appreciation for good design. I remember that every day he wore a crisp white short-sleeved, button-down, collared shirt. My grandmother, Celia, from Mexico, is a vivacious and stylish woman who comes from a whole family of jewelers. The epitome of high style, she always wears the finest adornments, has her hair styled, and red lipstick and heels in place—rain or shine, no matter where she's going. On my mom's side, Grandma Baker indulged me with a sparkling bin of costume tiaras, bracelets, necklaces, and earrings, kept at her home in Lakewood, California. I spent the days between visits dreaming of digging into that trunk! She also had a beautiful collection of imported trinkets and furniture from the 1940s, '50s, and '60s that came to me when she passed away. I love and cherish every special piece.

Growing up, I learned that it's not about how much you spend, it's about how you choose to see things—and I learned to see beauty in every experience and appreciate the details. The furniture, textiles, lighting, and interiors of the late '60s and '70s in Southern California influenced my aesthetic sensibilities, from my dad's colorful surfing ponchos, surfboards, and woven Mexican beach blankets to the rows of Craftsman- and casita-style bungalows I used to see as we rode through the city in our VW bus. And, thanks to my grandmothers, I learned at a very young age to love costume jewelry and "dressing up." Sparkling earrings and gold pendant necklaces were a part of my playground ensemble, and I still wear them today.

I studied design formally in the architecture program at Arizona State University, achieving a degree in interior design. The desert has its charms, but I just had to get back to the coast. Los Angeles has a rich history and its own special brand of nostalgia that brings me such joy. For me, Southern California is infused with an essence of hope, opportunity, beauty, and the feeling that this is where dreams come true.

When I met Ron, we were both at growth stages with our own businesses. We each had thought about opening a storefront to house the interesting collections of home décor that we just didn't have enough room for; we agreed that it would be nice to work together to showcase and sell some of this great stuff. Everything happened like magic. Even finding the space was serendipitous: We discovered the abandoned, run-down beauty salon next to a high-end antique showroom and gallery that Ron and I both frequented. We tracked down the landlord and wouldn't leave her alone. One of the partners in the antique gallery, Philip Stites, talked us up so much to the landlord that she eventually grew very keen on us. Before long, the space was ours, and the House of Design moved in, white picket fence and all.

opposite, top

Jaime's mom, Carolyn, on a beach in Rocky Point, 1973; Jaime's dad, Mike, with brother Sam in VW van, 1978.

opposite, middle

Grandma Celia and Grandpa Sam's house on Wilton Place, 1950s; Jaime and Dad, 1978; Jaime already into drapery at a young age, with brother Sam, 1970s; Mom and Grandma Baker, 1971.

opposite, bottom

Grandma Celia and Grandpa Sam's wedding day, 1943; Sam and Grandma Celia on eccentric leopard print furniture, 1950s; Jaime at age 5, the beginning of her love affair with hot hair rollers, 1979.

below, left to right

Grandma Celia as a young beauty, 1940s; Grandpa Sam in the Italian navy, 1940s; Jaime at green plastic desk with pants to match, 1976; Jaime and her hippy parents enjoying wide open spaces, 1975.

WHAT'S INSIDE

Have you ever opened a design magazine and wondered, How did they do that? We think it's unfair not to share. Throughout this book, we will share our design philosophy, our approach to interiors, and some tricks of the trade. Alongside gorgeous photographs of individual items and completed spaces will be stories about the many people we work with and where our inspiration comes from. We'll explain our take on pattern, scale, color, texture, and proportion, and we'll illustrate how and when to apply these basic elements of design to create dynamic, surprising, glamorous living spaces. Once we've defined the concepts that form the basis of our design sense, we'll show you how we've applied them to private homes and special projects. Doodles, sketches, collages of photos and fabric swatches, and many revisions of an idea help us come to the final well-planned conclusions, so we'll show these side by side with the result.

We hope you will find *High Style* an inspiring guide to enriching your everyday life. In it you'll see some of Southern California's hidden gems, as well as its secrets to stylish living, through our eyes. But you can live like a star no matter where you call home, and we'll show you how. Join us on a journey of stylish living!

opposite

We use our storefront window as a mini-installation, just a taste to entice passersby.

following pages

Ron and Jaime take a moment to enjoy their living room installation featuring Florence Broadhurst wallpaper and textiles.

Making It Work

Have you ever walked into a room that just felt right or visited a home so comfortable that you didn't want to leave? The hosts of these spaces won you over subconsciously because they properly incorporated and combined the basic elements of design. When these principles are used properly, the result is anything but plain. Learn to use these tools and your home decorating will be head and shoulders above the rest.

Some folks may think interior design is arbitrary, an art form subject to individual preferences. But good decorating is not only based on having creative sense and a good eye—it also incorporates a kind of science. Even if your look is eclectic, it's not about throwing things together at random. A great space tells the story of the people who spend time there. Put together correctly, you have a space that communicates peace, joy, and comfort in living. But used improperly, those same elements result in a feeling of fragmentation and dis-comfort—just plain bad design!

We believe interior design is the expression of the relation-ships between pattern, scale, color, texture, and proportion, and that an interesting, vibrant, and harmonious living space explores these relationships. It's true that there are a lot of artsy individuals out there, and many have a naturally good eye or a talent for flea market finds. But all too often, people just mix things together and decide they have a "design." Many people are used to thinking about color, and maybe about pattern, too, but it's attention to texture, proportion, and scale that makes a room inviting as well. In this chapter we will outline these basic elements.

previous pages, left

A warm, sumptuous master bedroom suite in Woodson & Rummerfield's Micheltorena Street project.

previous pages, right

Woodson & Rummerfield's Chrysanthemum wallpaper pattern, rendered in black-on-black.

left, top

Surprising decorations, like this porcelain bird adorning a vintage glass by Georges Briard, give a room personality.

left, bottom

A tasteful grouping of vintage artwork, by artists including Edward Goodall (1893) and George Gobo (early 1900s), look great together thanks to the changes in scale and proportion of small items to large ones.

opposite

The circles of Woodson & Rummerfield's Sunset Mirror echo the rounded edges of the furniture in this breezy entryway. The off-white accent color ties the pieces together and lets them stand out against the fresh color of the wall behind.

34

PATTERN

A pattern is a repeated decorative design or series of images. This can be anything from a simple stripe to a playful, stylized floral. Since patterns go in and out of style all the time, many patterns are associated with particular eras or cultures. We are partial to bold stripes and prints that incorporate large urns, garlands, trellises, or most anything that evokes the Belle Époque. (Belle Époque means "beautiful era" in French and signifies a period stretching from the late 1800s to World War I.) We also love patterns with whimsical and strong graphic elements. People often shy away from large or wild patterns and go for smaller, subtle prints, but these tend to fade together and die in a large room, and the pattern is lost. Don't worry about being too brash or intense—in a composition, a good-sized pattern adds more visual interest.

previous pages, left

A 1970s chandelier illuminates this dining room at twilight. Lucite dining chairs and mod art pieces stand out against the rain-wash walls and laid-back natural colors and materials of the décor.

previous pages, top right

The bar in the Great Room at the Esquire Showcase house is the epitome of posh with its flocked Griffin wallpapered niches and crisp white Roman urns.

previous pages, bottom right

Soft lighting, natural colors and textures, and a scenic view of Los Feliz make this a warm and welcoming room.

opposite

A delightful spotted floral pattern by Florence Broadhurst.

below

Patterns are a great way to bring excitement to a room, and you can have a lot of fun mixing them up. Patterns come in a wide variety–everything from tone-on-tone and colorful designs, to bold, repeating shapes.

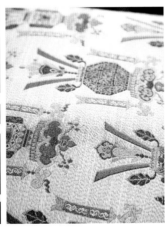

SCALE

Scale refers to how large or small a pattern or object appears. We prefer larger-scaled patterns when it comes to fabrics and wallpapers; such patterns add that extra "wow" factor. When mixing patterns, it's key to incorporate extreme scales in order to keep the prints from competing. For example, we might use a toile pattern on a sofa and pair it with wallpaper that has a small stripe or a very large graphic Damask pattern. Incorporating scale allows there to be variety without competition between prints.

below, left to right

A large-scale artichoke pattern complemented by a series of stripes in the same color scheme. A powder room in large-scale pink Kabuki Fan wallpaper.

opposite

A palette of pink, gold, citrus green, and black in a multitude of different scales adds a touch of whimsy to a room.

COLOR

When we talk about color we're refering to the science and logic behind hues (gradation of color—such a blue-reds and orange-reds), tints (lighter hues—colors with more white, such as sky blue), shades (darker hues—colors with more black, such as blue danube), and values (the degree of saturation in a color) of the color spectrum. Don't let color intimidate you! Adding color makes all the difference in a space, and yes, white is a color, too. When trying to choose color, some people automatically gravitate toward the lightest hues because they're afraid their walls will end up too bright. But we think saturated colors are gorgeous and impact-ful. Use a fan-deck of colors from the paint store to help you choose—the middle color of each fan-deck page is the middle-of-the-road color. Moving upward, white is added to create lighter tints. Moving downward, black is added to the same color to create darker shades. Colors of the same value always work well together. We like contrast, so usually we'll choose one really striking color to drive the whole project, then use more subtle hints and accent tones in the same value to support it. This helps bridge the colors, linking the scheme together.

opposite

This beach bungalow balances sophistication and relaxation with a dynamic combi-nation of hazel and leapfrog green, accented by punches of black and white.

below

Whenever possible, avoid using individual sample cards to choose colors. If you look at a color on a fan-deck, you may find that the red you singled out is actually more pink or purple than you thought when you viewed it on its own.

following pages

With so many bold colors, patterns, and textures, this dining room could be overwhelming. But because the design elements are used correctly, the result is a powerful yet harmonious statement.

TEXTURE

Texture is the feel, appearance, or consistency of a surface
or material. People often forget to consider texture. There
are a multitude of classic textures to choose from. We love
the feel of a lush mohair, the nubbiness of a well-made
bouclé, a silk velvet with luster, a tailored woven linen,
and loomed wools. The more texture you can incorporate
by mixing and matching, the more tactile interest you'll
achieve. People tend to resort to the same materials for
everything in the room, and it just leaves you flat. But textures don't clash the way other elements might—the more
variety, the merrier. For example, you can use the same
color over and over with different textures, which looks
very smart, but using the same material over and over is just
bland, especially in the same color.

opposite, top

*Smooth, shiny chrome nail heads combined with a faux zebra fur pillow make this
velvet chair a soft and stylish seating experience.*

opposite, bottom

*A soft, velvety pillow in rich colors provides the perfect background for this raised,
highly textured, hand-stitched pheasant; the result beckons to be touched.*

below, left to right

*A nubby bouclé; a shaggy wool rug and woven textiles; a soft cashmere print; a
rough, natural basket weave.*

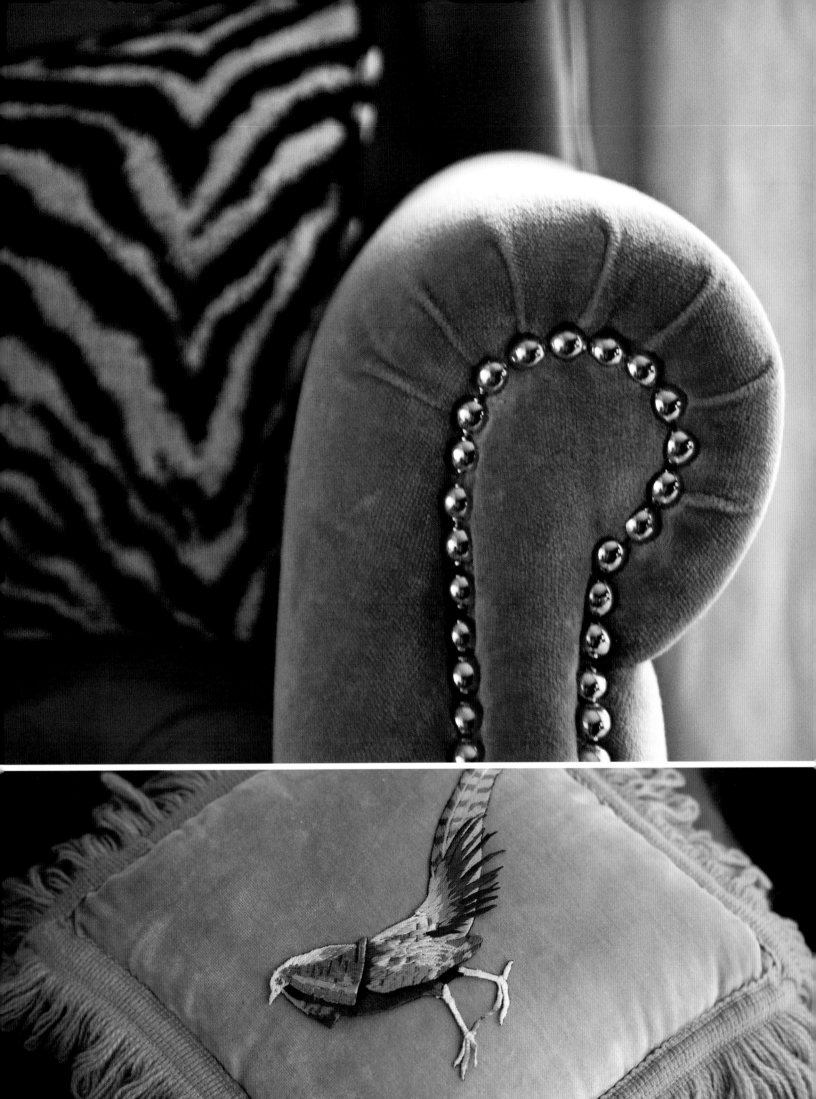

PROPORTION

Proportion is the relationship of one object to another in terms of size and quantity. A good ratio to remember is the golden ratio (where the sum of two quantities is to the larger quantity as the larger quantity is to the smaller), which in turn yields the golden section. When in doubt, go with a 1-to-1.6 ratio. For example, say you are designing a headboard. A good start would be to take the width of the bed and divide it in half. This number will result in a height for the headboard that is aesthetically pleasing.

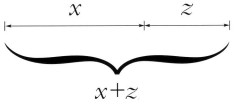

$$x+z \text{ IS TO } x \text{ AS } x \text{ IS TO } z$$

If you have a huge, cavernous room, don't cluster a few tiny pieces in the middle and hope no one notices the misuse of volume—add large artwork and taller plants. Likewise, if you have a small room, don't fill it up with big, bulky, dark leather furniture. A great composition is ultimately about the relationship between objects, and good proportion is achieved when there is balance and harmony in those relationships. But you'll have more interaction with your environment if each of those objects has its own personality. It's easy to opt for furniture collections where you can feel secure knowing that everything matches, but the most fabulous rooms are composed of a variety of sizes and shapes, creating interest and flow. For example, combine a pair of delicate, open-air leg chairs with a good-sized, low-to-the-floor sofa. Different back heights and variety of furniture-leg lengths add interest.

opposite
A nicely proportioned headboard and lampshades give this room a beautiful balance.

below
Since the Renaissance, artists and architects such as Leonardo da Vinci, Vitruvius, and Le Corbusier have proportioned their works according to the Golden Ratio—a geometric system, based on the human body, that guides perfect proportion, which is generally considered aesthetically pleasing. Le Corbusier's "Le Modular" is a diagram of a man of proportions that utilizes the Golden Ratio.

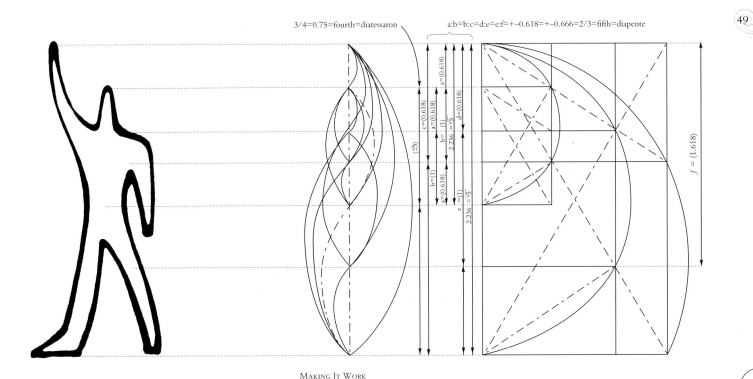

SHADOW PLAY
Be inspired by the lengthening shadows of winter to create a magical world of silhouettes and trompe l'oeil murals — all in a dramatic black and white palette.
By Amanda Kaiser. Photographer Craig Knowles.

À LONDRES, LA CRÈME DES BEIGES

Chic

THOMAS O'BRIEN TEXTILES

the new mandarins

inner sanctum

From Point A to Point B

When starting a design project, first we take into account the client's needs and wishes and then consider the context of the site and/or the objects to be incorporated. It's important for us to know where items came from or what the home's history is because that information informs our decisions. Then we think about what we want to say with the project and what the space is asking for. For us, it's about creating an experience, an overarching concept also referred to as *partée* by those in the design world.

Next, we start putting out feelers for objects and elements that strike the right chords. Like many designers, we create "mood boards," both for the project as a whole and for each room. Mood boards are a part of our road map; they help us set the tone, and they're visual aids to creating a common vocabulary so that everyone involved is speaking the same language. You'd be surprised how many different ideas clients would have if we just said, "We're going to go with a modern French look," without showing images to explain our concept. We combine our boards with sketches, floor plans, and renderings to create a visual language.

As we create the mood boards, we talk with our clients about what they like and what we like. It's equally important to know what the clients don't like, as that helps us refine the functional and decorative aspects of a space. At first, the road map is an overarching concept: When we're looking for inspirations and influences, we're pulling together images of everything from lighting to wallpaper to colors to furniture to scenes from movies to clippings from magazines. Planning is where we spend the most time. We like to have most everything figured out before we pull the trigger.

Plus, working with a plan helps us look at the project as a whole. Most of our clients don't think to question their existing floor plan or even where else they could put the fridge. Knocking down a wall or moving a window can change a space dramatically. Once you learn to open your eyes to those possibilities, some really wonderful outcomes are realized.

As we scheme and shop, the mood board images start getting replaced with pictures of the actual items we plan to use. In addition to the look and feel of our choices, we also consider lead time and price point. All this research and coordination has to happen first so that we don't get halfway done with a project and then realize that the sofas won't be ready until months later. Finally, we create spreadsheets that we use like shopping lists; we print them out, stick them in our tote bags, and hit the streets.

opposite, top
A vintage room rendering by Helen Edel Sloan from 1962.

opposite, bottom
Visual aids, such as this mood board with inspirations and furniture layout schematics, help the designer and client maintain a common visual vocabulary.

51

Somewhere in between the beginning and the finale of a project is where we believe the magic happens—the design process gives birth to many pleasant discoveries. Sometimes, despite careful preparation, you find yourself in a situation you hadn't planned on. You might have settled on all the furniture for the living room before realizing, You know, this settee would be amazing in the foyer. The design process is like working on a puzzle: The actual picture only comes to life when you dive in and start putting the pieces together.

Unexpected details in your home are like jewelry—the perfect one can finish an ensemble in just the right way. This chinois-style chair back below, with its faux-bamboo details, diamond pattern, and punch of color, is candy for the eye. The spectacular Mattia Biagi sculpture, a toy gun dipped in tar, adds dimension to a solid wall.

opposite
The finishing touches on a delightful room with a modern palette of red, black, and white.

below, left to right
Chinois-style chair back with bamboo detail; Mattia Biagi's "Tar Gun" sculpture; Ron and Jaime with artist Mattia Biagi.

following pages
Yet another iteration of a grand living room at Woodson & Rummerfield's boutique featuring a fresh take on traditional forms using very future-forward textiles. We used one of our favorite techniques for instant impact: a black and white palette with accents of one bold color.

The Road Map

Always consider your choices for color, texture, and pattern together. Pick a palette of colors. Mix things up with different materials, fabric styles, and finish types, but make sure your pattern choices coordinate with respect to their scales and color families. And don't forget to use a variety of scales and proportions when choosing and placing your furniture and objects! Once you are happy with it, remember to stick to your road map, but allow yourself to make adjustments for magical intervention.

opposite

Lighting is a big consideration when creating a design. Ambient light is warm and inviting. Achieve the glow with table lamps, and use dimmers on overhead lighting as much as possible. And remember, don't overuse light—in this case a dim bulb is a good thing. Keep plenty of soft 45-watt bulbs on hand to create a perfect soft glow, as seen here from this elegant wall sconce. The thin stripes of the custom shade are fabulous against the large-scale pattern of the wallpaper behind it.

"How can we develop taste? Some of us, alas, can never develop it, because we can never let go of shams. We must learn to recognize suitability and proportion, and apply our knowledge to our needs. I grant you we may never fully appreciate the full balance of proportion but we can exert our common sense and decide whether a thing is suitable. A technical knowledge of architecture is not necessary to know that a huge stuffed leather chair in a tiny gold and cream room is unsuitable, is hideously complicated, and is much out of proportion as the proverbial bull in the china shop". —Elsie de Wolfe, *The House in Good Taste.*

The House In Good Taste

HIGH STYLE AT ITS FINEST

In 2006, we collaborated with creative mastermind Alan Rohwer on designing two rooms for Versace, to help raise money for various charities, at the *Esquire* magazine Showcase House—a 17,000-square-foot home in Beverly Hills. The annual showcase pairs up designers to create a backdrop worthy of a star-studded charity auction. This particular showcase was an invitation-only event, with such high-profile guests as Pierce Brosnan, Felicity Huffman, Minnie Driver, Salma Hayek, Kirsten Dunst, Ben Affleck, Jennifer Garner, Jason Bateman, Clive Davis, Janet Jackson, Stevie Wonder, and Randy Jackson, to name just a few.

For the *partée*, we developed the theme "Milan meets Los Angeles," inspired by couture fashion and high design. Like the two cities, this room—which features items from the Versace furniture collection—is dynamic, grand, and world-class. The contrasts are dramatic, with a modern Renaissance flair. This space is sleek beyond sleek, exquisite like a perfectly tailored suit, yet it remains luxuriously comfortable.

In the Great Room, a highly textured white shag rug provides a foundation of softness and luxury for the svelte Versace leather sofas and club chairs and the gleaming chrome-and-smoked-glass tables. The focal point—a backlit, white onyx fireplace—glows with warm gold undertones, which bring out the espresso and violet accents in the room and help them stand out against the cool black-and-white palette. The Venetian plaster on the walls is a subtle, suede gray, adding richness to the room; the airy, white silk drapes float over it like fluffy, voluptuous clouds. With their deep plum–colored ribbon edging and gentle sheen, the drapes

soften the hard angles and resilient surfaces of the furniture. For interest, the white couture sofas and club chairs feature a subtle Greek key pattern—synonymous with the Versace brand   on the arms. Adjacent to the living space is a smart and sophisticated reading area, for immersing oneself in a classic tome. The variegated shape of the stones in the rock-crystal lamp bases contrasts nicely with the polished surface of the monolithic glass-and-chrome Versace desk.

The bar at the end of this grand room features a wonderful, large-scaled red "griffin" pattern on black wallpaper with a dramatic, velvety finish. The real find of the project was a pair of antique acanthus-leaf sconces from Argentina, which are reminiscent of a detail in the Joan Crawford movie *The Women*, and that give the room some historic glamour. The space is a chic palette of high-couture black-and-white furnishings with cool chrome and glass accents, and the interior architecture's deep plum, brown, and gold finishing adds warmth for a wonderful balance. The essence of the space is sophisticated, intelligent, and welcoming. This was the most popular room in the house during the events.

opposite, top left
Sculptured vintage lighting with amber bulbs adds warmth and romance to a room.

opposite, bottom, left to right
Jaime and Ron with Gavin de Graw; Randy Jackson; and Jadrian Johnson.

below, left to right
Jaime and Ron with Liz Phair; Ted Danson and Mary Steenburgen; designer Sami Hayek.

I Love L.A.

Los Angeles is a design-inspiration mecca. Whether you're lounging at the beach or shopping on trendy Robertson Boulevard, you'll find yourself surrounded by a wide variety of interesting perspectives portrayed through art, architecture, and clothing. Fashion is a big part of the Los Angeles scene, and Angelenos have mastered this most outward form of expression. The "fashion forecast" for clothing is parallel to that of the interior design world; we are constantly inspired by fashion, whether by a scarf, brooch, or herringbone-patterned coat. The city is made up of a diverse and colorful array of culture and style, which creates an atmosphere of openness, limitlessness, and cutting-edge possibility.

Having a beach nearby changes your lifestyle—enjoyment in the outdoors is relished here to a greater degree than in many other large cities. Living in Los Angeles, you can't help but luxuriate in the sunshine. It makes you want to put the convertible top down, pull your leather driving gloves on, wrap a colorful scarf around your hair, and take off for a weekend excursion to another SoCal destination, like nearby Malibu or Palm Springs. When the sun goes down, aptly named Sunset Boulevard takes over as the pulse of the city; Angelenos head to the boulevard to celebrate life and share the warm night air with friends and loved ones at any number of restaurants and clubs. Angelenos love the scene and to be seen.

Like our clients, each neighborhood of L.A. is very different from the next. To the west lie the beachside communities known for their quaint Craftsman-style bungalows and ocean views, while Malibu and the Pacific Palisades feature grand cliffside estates that rival the ocean's splendor. Famous Beverly Hills and Bel Air to the north are favorite showcases for Old Hollywood flavor, preserved in the Regency estates' heavy-timber wood moldings, elegant stone reliefs, and French castlelike facades. At the center of it all, the Hollywood Hills feature some fabulous mid-century modern homes with clean lines and sophisticated style. Toward the east, Silver Lake's Mediterranean-inspired homes, with their Spanish-style tile roofs (a Southern California trademark) commingling with the modern lines of the '50s and '60s, give shape to an eclectic, artistic neighborhood. You can learn a lot about L.A. by studying its architecture, much of it designed or inspired by great visionaries, such as Frank Lloyd Wright, Rudolf Schindler, and Richard Neutra.

Decades of silver-screen Hollywood glamour still shine through the veneer of the many old buildings—especially theaters—around town. In fact, a lot of old elements have survived the transition to modern day. A walk around Los Angeles will reveal sconces, once lit with gas, flanking entryways to retail shops. You might see an old clocktower gracing the top of a regal building that now serves as a dry cleaner. Retro coffee shops and diners sit huddled between more modern constructs, a lasting connection to the dream of hometown U.S.A., built by Midwest transplants. The little boutiques, each with their own character, are often housed in buildings with old stone facades, so familiar to anyone who's lived in L.A. Palm trees planted decades ago still line the roads and punctuate the lush colors of the hills. Everywhere you turn, you can see the face of L.A. as it's been through the eras; it's this synergy of the old and the new that creates the unique vibration of creative energy that feeds our work.

What we choose to see about L.A. is that the city is permeated with hope and optimism—this really is the land of opportunity, a place where people come to make their dreams come true. People here embrace the past, perhaps in part because it reminds us of the enduring power of those dreams. We're very involved in the restoration and conservation of L.A., a reflection of our love affair with the City of Angels.

previous pages, left
Ron and Jaime cruising Pacific Coast Highway in Malibu.

previous pages, right
Florence Broadhurst's Bird of Paradise pattern, rendered in black-on-black.

below, left
Who wouldn't be inspired by this glorious sunset over Point Dume?

below, right
A sunny, windswept picnic at Zuma Beach gives good vibrations.

opposite
Jaime and Ron can often be seen enjoying L.A. in high style—in this case, behind the wheel of a 1999 Ferrari 550 Maranello.

PURIST SENSIBILITIES

Driving up to the historic central neighborhood of Hollywood, at the intersection of Franklin and Gower, and meandering into the hills, you'll find a restoration project of ours known as the Bonnet House, a modern architectural landmark designed by Richard Neutra and built in 1941—the first of many redwood, stucco, and glass homes by this pioneer architect of modernism. In Barbara Lamprecht's book, *Neutra: The Complete Works*, there is a photograph of this home, built for Ted Bonnet and nestled into the remote hillside, nothing but brush around it. Today the house is surrounded by numerous styles of homes, all butting up against one another. The times sure have changed.

Though he worked on a handful of commercial and government spaces, Richard Neutra's true legacy is the hundreds of modern, streamline-styled residences he designed, many of the homes still making a statement in neighborhoods across the country. He will forever be known for defining and pioneering the modern architectural movement, which he started right here in Los Angeles. Neutra homes are some of the most sought-after pieces of architecture in the world. Never mind the Jean Prouvé tables and Picasso paintings: To really be of the moment, why not collect a piece of trophy property? The name of one's architect or pedigree of property carries a lot of clout in L.A., just as brand-name jeans or an expensive car does. You can imagine the accordingly lofty price of a Neutra, but the inhabitant of the Bonnet House may surprise you. Is he an architect, like Neutra? A high-profile surgeon? A famous writer? Try a retired hard-core punk musician, now a senior advertising and marketing executive.

To us, it seems quite fitting that this exemplary home is owned by Jonathan Anastas, a true modern-day design enthusiast. He only wants the best of the best, no skimping allowed. From vintage decorative arts to lighting fixtures to outdoor furniture, each piece that Jonathan purchases and showcases in his home absolutely must have a pedigree or story to tell, just like the house itself. Originals only, please, no interpretations. He is what we consider a purist. And because he was already so high-style, our objective in designing his interior was to add more substance and character to the space, which had become a beautiful but rather limited collection of modernist, buzzword brand names, such as the "big three": Eames, van der Rohe, and Nelson.

previous pages
Poolside is the best way to enjoy the views in the Hollywood Hills.

opposite, top
Showcasing an original design by architect Richard Neutra, the home affords fantastic views of the hills beyond from the large porch, which was designed for just this purpose.

opposite, bottom
Richard Neutra's Bonnet House in Hollywood is comprised of a trio of cubes angled into the hillside and topped by a sloping roof-line. Neutra's unique, modern approach to architecture was hailed by critics and earned this house accolades upon its completion in 1942.

below, left to right
Jonathan, Ron, and Jaime enjoy a cocktail on the porch at the Bonnet House. The home retains its original wood siding, a beautiful red wood tone that we repeated inside the house with similarly colored paint. Floor-to-ceiling windows make the perfect backdrop to a beautifully set table, ready for entertaining.

All the Paul McCobb Planner Group furniture in the house was Jonathan's grandfather's—purchased from the original line at its launch in the early 1950s. The furniture first resided in the Winchester, Massachusetts, home his grandfather had built by Robert Woods Kennedy (a Harvard colleague of Bauhaus founder Walter Gropius), who wrote *The House and the Art of Its Design*. The furniture traveled from Massachusetts to Jonathan's parents' more traditional home, and then on to a more appropriate setting in Jonathan's Neutra house in Los Angeles. Shown in the living room is a McCobb end table with a Tom Ford coffee-table book.

JOURNEY OF AN OBJECT

When you move about in high-design circles and pay attention to the media of luxury living, you learn pretty quickly which name brands are considered chic and of the moment. It's no crime to invest in these pieces—they are often beautiful and of a high quality. But style becomes more personal when you take the time to research an era or a certain look that speaks to you. Open a book on the modern history of design, decorative arts, or furniture, and you'll get an overview of the biggest, most recognizable names. Our challenge to Jonathan was to go beyond the brands he'd learned to associate with high style and explore more unique, noteworthy items for his collection of furnishings. Once you look more closely and do a little shopping, you'll find a wealth of trusted names that aren't being tossed about in every design magazine. In fact, the primary job of a well-curated furniture shop is to introduce you to high-end brands and less well-known items that have astonishing histories or have received accolades. Once you start comparing products and pieces, you'll learn to see the merit behind the work. Researching a lesser-known designer might reveal that he is critically acclaimed and has a loyal following, so even though he might not be buzz-worthy at the moment, the credibility is clear.

When Jonathan purchased the Bonnet House, it was in a bit of disrepair. We wanted to maintain the integrity of the period architecture but also to incorporate a high standard of 21st-century living. What interests Jonathan is the blend of Bauhaus modern and old-world luxury brands: high-tech and over-the-top quality meet clean lines, the function unimpeded by the form. We called our concept for Jonathan's Neutra "organic modern"; we used a lot of natural materials and colors, which were offset by contemporary photography and sexy lines to freshen up the look. The result is the perfect backdrop to showcase Jonathan's outrageous collections.

opposite

Neutra was among the first to use moveable walls of glass as doors, an innovation that facilitated the concept of indoor-outdoor living, such as these glass walls leading to the front porch of the Bonnet House.

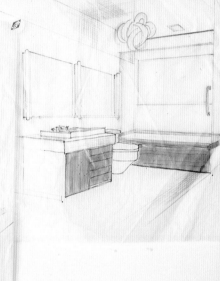

previous pages

With its natural finishes and neutral palette, this "organic modern" dining room is the perfect showcase for the owner's unique decorative arts and noteworthy embellishments, such as the pop-era Verner Panton hanging light fixture.

above, clockwise from top left

Mood boards for our restoration of the Bonnet House show a study of organic and fashion paint palettes. These bathroom and kitchen concept renderings are part of our Road Map and help us to plan and stay on track when designing a project.

opposite, top

This restored living room stays true to its roots with Neutra's original finishes, such as the Douglas fir wall paneling and aluminum-style ribbon windows. This arrangement of modern pedigreed pieces has great proportion: these smallish, vintage wood chairs by Edmond Spence are light and open next to the solid, Karl Springer plinth base coffee table. The overarching Arco floor lamp frames the furniture vignette.

opposite, bottom

The textures of the nubby wool rug and smooth leather Barcelona chairs contrast nicely and help define the living area from the sleek, shiny dining room.

The historic ARCO Center office building in downtown L.A. was redecorated in 1973 by Herbert Bayer, a founding member of the Bauhaus movement. When City National Bank bought the building in 2003, they gutted and tossed nearly everything. Luckily, some small, not-too-worn pieces of the wall-to-wall carpets, designed by Bayer, were cut into area rugs. Jonathan loves to shop and see what's new around town, and when he brought this rug to our attention, we fell in love with it! We applauded his feeling his way out of the box and admired the impactful design of the rug. The fact that it's a salvaged piece from a historic building makes it quite unique and perfectly Modage.

JOURNEY OF AN OBJECT

A renovation doesn't have to be a slavish reenactment of the past; it's more important to consider the spirit of the space as a whole. On this project, we wondered: If Neutra were alive today, would he use this material or piece of equipment? We updated aging, nonfunctioning items with durable modern-day equivalents, all the while sticking close to the home's original palette: stone, wood, and glass with a color palette of gold, amber, and earth and sunset tones. All equipment and appliances are top of the line and energy efficient. We kept the original cabinets and painted them a color called Intellectual Gray to add warmth. The walls are painted a redwood color that matches the exterior wood tone. The organic cork kitchen floor and Carrara marble countertops add natural textures, which contrast nicely with the modern light fixtures; the ceiling is peppered with three light fixtures by Arne Jacobsen for Louis Poulsen: two "Beehive" lights and a pendant, called Oslo, over the sink.

The living and dining rooms have original finishes per Neutra's specifications, with Douglas fir wood paneling, a painted brick fireplace, and aluminum-style ribbon windows with a sliding-glass wall. These two rooms are actually different sides of one larger space, so we used a neutral white tone on the walls throughout to keep the room feeling open and light and to connect the two rooms visually. The living room features Karl Springer elements and Bauhaus influences, mixed with some of the aforementioned big three, such as the leather Mies van der Rohe Barcelona chairs. The materials give a very natural vibe: lots of buttery leather, wood grain, and woven textures. The large pattern of the napped rug helps anchor the rest of the furnishings in the living room and kicks up the scales and textures of the room composition. For the dining room, we brought in the Verner Panton light fixture, which we suspended above a T. H. Robsjohn-Gibbings dining table, surrounded by 1970s molded Lucite chairs, called Flou, in the color Smoke. The sleek, shiny finishes of the light fixture, table, and chairs reflect the light flowing throughout the room.

opposite, clockwise from top left

These chairs by Edmond Spence are made of wood and natural, un-dyed woven material: very organic modern. Cork floors and natural light warm up the modern elements of the kitchen. The sleek, shiny finishes of this T.H. Robs-John Gibbings dining table and smoked Lucite "Flou" chairs stand out as a separate "room" next to the more tactile and natural surfaces in the living room area. The translucent materials maximize the effect of the light that shines all day through the large windows and glass walls.

Jonathan's fine- and decorative-art collection has emerged as one of our favorites of all time. This wall adjacent to the dining room has become something of a relics display. The array of found objects is very interesting, even provoking. Up against the wall rests a unique Springer console table and two incredible Billy Haines ottomans with sterling-silver leg tips nestled underneath. On top of the console is an extremely rare pair of once-controversial Italian "blacka-moor" candlestick holders from the 1940s, depicting slaves, posturing next to the Mattia Biagi Cristo standing crucifix. Then there's the black-bronze horse head—a classic, powerful, masculine image captured with surprising grace. All of this sits below a huge photo of legendary L.A. skateboarder Tony Alva. And it works, because all of these things speak to Jonathan and collectively represent him well. We relish in the fact that living space is such a fantastic outlet for expression. In fact, it's because of this expressiveness that the space is alive. Projects like this remind us why we do what we do.

The Bonnet House has a wonderful westward patio exposure and is fantastic for sunset entertaining. The golden sun slowly sets over the vistas and palm trees in the distance. You can even see the unmistakable round roofline of the Capitol Records building. Jonathan often entertains high-profile actors and producers from "the Biz" and all sorts of design enthusiasts. The mingling and canoodling amongst the designer furnishings and vintage barware, with the rattle of the cocktail shaker continuing late into the evening, is just how you might imagine a party in the Hollywood Hills would be. To Jonathan, it is just another night—he's already thinking about his morning routine and wondering what news tomorrow's paper will bring.

previous pages

An Hermès tray houses some of Jonathan's cufflinks and other fine jewelry from Chrome Hearts.

below, left to right

Chrome Hearts' sterling silver belt buckle; vintage ceramic Blackamoor candlestick holder, books from Jonathan's personal library, with a Chrome Hearts sterling silver wallet chain.

opposite

Jonathan's fine- and decorative-art collection has emerged as one of our favorites of all time. This wall adjacent to the dining room has become something of a relics display. The array of found objects is very interesting, even thought-provoking. Against the wall rests a unique Springer console table and two incredible Billy Haines ottomans with sterling silver leg tips nestled underneath. On top of the console is an extremely rare pair of Italian Blackamoor candlestick holders from the 1940s, posturing next to the Mattia Biagi Cristo standing crucifix. Then there's the black-bronze horse head—a classic, powerful, masculine image captured with surprising grace. All of this sits below a huge photo of legendary L.A. skateboarder Tony Alva. And it works because all of these things speak to Jonathan and collectively represent him well.

opposite, above, and following pages

Jonathan's jewel box of a bathroom was completely updated with gold and amber mosaic tiles, mirrored walls, Flos lighting, and Philippe Starck fixtures. It is quite a sexy bathroom—complete with a window wall from the shower to the outdoors and a floor-to-ceiling mirrored wall. All the surfaces are smooth and reflective to take advantage of the indoor/outdoor feel provided by the view out to the adjacent tropical landscaping. The tiny square tiles—perfectly scaled for the small room and arranged in a randomized pattern—are an iridescent array of colors that gives a warm ambience.

previous pages

We often find design inspiration in the fashion trends from the past and today. We love how the simple black diamond-lattice fishnets are working with the animal print of this skirt. Neutral colors keep the combo classy.

opposite

Modage invites you to inject fun and flair into your everyday life. This high-style cocktail is served in a vintage highball glass from Woodson and Rummerfield's House of Design.

below, counter clockwise from top

This spectacular view from the front porch of the Bonnet House is enjoyed by Jonathan's guests, such as these tattooed party-goers wearing rare vintage skater T-shirts from "Go Monkey Business." Ron, Jonathan, and Jaime enjoy a summer evening cocktail party.

CREATIVE DOMICILE

Laurel Canyon originated in the early 1900s as a road for the trackless electric trolley that ran up the canyon to the top of Lookout Mountain. The shady canyon sheltered a sleepy community, peppered with small bungalows, shacks, and your occasional compound, where eccentrics, such as silent-film star Tom Mix and magician Harry Houdini, gathered to share artistic communion. Today, Laurel Canyon has emerged as the most legendary of all L.A.'s canyon neighborhoods. Because of its central location, people from all around Los Angeles know it as a favorite shortcut, driving through it over the Mulholland Ridge to the Valley. The shacks have given way to a higher standard of living, but many of the bungalows remain, flanking streets haunted by memories of rock legends like Jim Morrison, Frank Zappa, The Byrds, and Joni Mitchell.

Located a stone's throw from the old Canyon market and Pace restaurant—the favorite and only pit stop in the canyon, famous for its rustic Euro influence and great food—sits our clients' three-level home from the 1970s. Suzanne Marques and Robert Dourisboure both work in television, and for them—like the entertainment legends of the past—their house in the canyon is a place to escape from the intensity of their careers. But before the house could become the chic retreat they envisioned, it needed some work. First and foremost, our clients needed a place that really felt like home. We wanted all those who would enter their home to be so pleased by the smart, tasteful, and whimsical space that they'd stay awhile. Now that we have had a design intervention, they have that—a home that is impressive yet comfortable, every curve and texture beckoning visitors to relax in artistic sophistication.

below

Laurel Canyon Boulevard and a trackless trolley in Laurel Canyon at Sunset Boulevard at the turn of the century.

opposite

This entry into our Laurel Canyon project welcomes visitors with bright, whimsical blue walls and tiled floors. The unique curve of the staircase is emphasized by the contrasting white trim, a curved banister, and a collection of framed images in an assortment of sizes and shapes along the wall.

There are parts of classic 1970s L.A. décor that we would prefer to leave in the past, but in order to stay true to the era of the house, we decided to bring in some strong period-design elements. Both Robert and Suzanne are big collectors of contemporary art and are quite fashion forward, so we went wild. We found our inspiration in the work of Karl Springer, Florence Broadhurst, and the late fashion designer Halston. Karl Springer was known in the '70s for his high-end furniture, ivory collectibles, and decorative lighting made of chrome and glass; his quirky exotic designs were high points of the era. Halston's chic fashion flair—beaded tunics, billowing caftans, halter pantsuits, and Ultrasuede shirtdresses with masterful cuts and detailing—and ad campaigns were extremely flashy, but timeless. Suzanne leans stylistically more toward traditional items and high-style fashion, so we incorporated some Regency nods, such as the black-and-white entertainment unit from our Modage collection. The Broadhurst wallpaper we chose to use in several rooms also invokes the Regency period.

opposite
An illuminated light fixture creates dramatic shadows.

below
Vintage Murano glassware shines in the sunlight.

following pages
In this living room, the LaChapelle photograph above the fireplace acts as a unifying element by tying in all of the colors of the house. With such vibrant artwork, we had freedom to manipulate the different tones of blue, green, burnished gold, pink, and coral.

The house has practically no right angles; it's a three-story walk-up with a three-level spiral staircase. The main room had a strange boxy partition between the kitchen and living room that felt like a big barrier, so we removed it, opening up the area into one large, free-flowing space. This is the nucleus of the house, and we wanted to showcase it. Having an open multipurpose area works well for dining, cooking, hanging out, and entertaining. What we love best about the 1970s are the bold, graphic prints and shiny materials, epitomized by the work of wallpaper designer Florence Broadhurst. Her fabulous retro patterns gave us a unifying theme for the house and helped us anchor the high ceilings. During our research for this project, we pulled a bunch of old decorating books from the '70s and saw a shot with this Circles and Squares Broadhurst pattern—we knew right away that it would perfectly cinch our concept for the living room. The geometric pattern provides a sense of order to combat the lack of structure in the open floor plan, and it also nicely reflects the shape of the spiral staircase. Continuing the theme, we used circle- and square-shaped furniture throughout the connected spaces.

We chose to complement the Circles and Squares wallpaper pattern in the living room with a large-scale-patterned custom rug. The colors in the woven wool rug are a wonderful bouquet of charcoal, sea grass, olive green, and twilight blue with a hint of white that just pops. The patterns in the wallpaper and rug go together very well without competing because of the change in scale. We dabbled with a few more small patterns, but the dynamic color scheme of all levels of green steals the show. The sofa is nice and boxy, tightly upholstered in a wonderful charcoal textile from a fashion collection by Paul Smith, with pin-striped suit pillows to match—the smooth, tailored fabric contrasts nicely with the soft, luxurious velvet side chairs and shimmery, flowing, floor-length drapes. The sofa is flanked by petite, brass, branch tables. The grouping has nice proportion: large sofa, small tables, oh so chic.

below, left
Brass with black and white lacquer is one of our favorite combinations.

below, right
Our discovery of this bold Florence Broadhurst Circles and Squares wallpaper inspired our design for the living room, which we executed in a custom color to better suit the owners' tastes.

opposite
This credenza designed by Woodson & Rummerfield's boasts a rich lacquered'sfinish with substantial oversized brass hardware.

following pages
Ron, Jaime, Patrick, Suzanne, and Robert enjoy an evening in the living room. The rounded and box-shaped living room furniture reflects the shapes of the Circles and Squares wallpaper, while its arrangement, grounded by the geometric patterned wool rug by Woodson & Rummerfield's, creates a sense of order. The changes in scale keep the dynamic patterns from clashing. The lacquered and mirrored coffee table, also by Woodson & Rummerfield's, is centered between the stand-out green chairs to bring balance to the room.

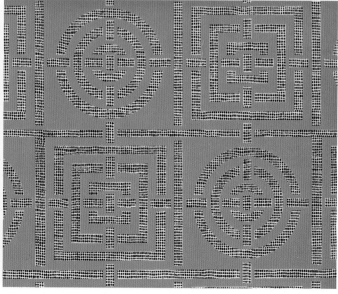

When we first met with Suzanne and Robert, we talked about what was important to them in order to get some design inspiration. Suzanne showed us their Tiffany china collection from their wedding, which had a wonderful vibrant green palm-leaf pattern. Moving forward from this first step, we chose a foiled wallpaper with a custom delicious green print to complement their sentimental china. We continued with an array of colors to balance the masculine and feminine throughout the home. The living room, kitchen, and dining area are a whimsical combination of greens and blues with pops of pink. A large-scaled fan-patterned wallpaper, called Kabuki, by Florence Broadhurst, carries the pink into the powder room. The play on scale is stunning.

Suzanne and Robert wanted their stylish guest room not only to make a statement but also to be welcoming and comfortable, so we went with the print called Cranes, also by Florence Broadhurst, in red on tan for the lamp shades, and combined this with a Chanel-inspired pattern in black and white for the headboard and draperies—which echoes the circles and squares vocabulary from the living room. The color combination and whimsical patterns are warm and inviting, an extension of the design in the rest of the home—this makes guests feel like part of the family and keeps the room from feeling like a hotel room, something separate and apart from the rest of the living spaces. Since we wanted the house to be chic and comfortable but were working with limited space, we selected very few pieces of furniture for the design and let the patterns make the visual punch. Suzanne and Robert are avid collectors of unique

and iconic artwork and photography, all of which gracefully adorn their newly designed home. The mantel features a David LaChapelle silk-screened piece called "Paris Vogue 1997," and throughout are works by Annie Leibovitz, Tim Burton, and David Lynch.

The dining table is a classic Florence Knoll piece, highlighted by a pair of "Shade Shade" chandeliers by Marcel Wanders for Moooi. The chandeliers and the starlike shadows they cast really bring the eye up and celebrate the volume of the space, as do the colorful glass objets d'art displayed above the cabinets. The drapery, with a shimmer of silver in a soft, nubby, blue bouclé, adds to the height and light of the rooms. Both sets of chairs feature geometric patterns reminiscent of the circles and squares from the living area; the open latticelike work of the dining chairs contrasts with the more substantial, upholstered seats around the kitchen island. Thin green and white rectangular tiles in a simple randomized pattern create an uneven, slightly rough backsplash against the smooth white surface of the cabinets.

below
Powder room with Kabuki Fan wallpaper.

opposite, top
A vintage palm leaf serving plate by Tiffany & Co.

opposite, bottom left
Colorful decoratives add whimsy and visual punch. These 1920s pheasant figurines in brilliant turquoise are candy for the eye.

opposite, bottom right
Lampshades are so often overlooked, but can be a great place to make a subtle statement, such as with this sleek black shade.

previous pages

This small guest bedroom makes the most of its size with a bold, graphic pattern by Robert Allen on the headboard and matching drapes. Custom lampshades in Florence Broadhurst's famous Crane pattern are perched on mirrored end tables; the light from the lamps reflects against the mirrored surfaces to give the room an added sparkle.

above, clockwise from top left

It's the way finishing touches work together that makes a standout room. The rectangular tiles of the kitchen backsplash add texture. Fresh flowers are a simple and beautiful way to bring life into a room—Suzanne prepares a bouquet for a vase; a pop of color from a curvy kettle contrasts with geometric tile on the backsplash.

opposite

The dining area is part of an open floor plan, so we continued the theme from the living room with more Circles and Squares wallpaper and a circular Eero Saarinen dining table surrounded by chairs with circle cutout chair backs. Overhead, a simultaneously vintage-and-modern-looking Moooi Shade chandelier gives the room a dash of Modage style.

following pages

Stainless steel appliances and white lacquered surfaces complemented by Woodson and Rummerfield's green and white barstools make this open kitchen and dining area both modern and deliciously retro at the same time.

BEVERLY HILLS: HOME TO THE STARS

Imagine an old Spanish estate with a mature landscape, a worn but immaculate cobblestone driveway, and purple wisteria swaying in the Beverly Hills breeze. Picture gardens growing beyond the house, up into the hills, and a menagerie of flowers and pruned trees that seem to go on forever. What a place to lose yourself in. As you enter, you immediately notice the Majorelle, Sue et Mar, and other Parisian and English antiques of the Art Nouveau and Art Deco eras. Exotic textiles with prints of dahlias, magnolias, pansies, lilacs, and roses cover chairs, tabletops, rugs, and lamps. Collections of Postimpressionist artwork from the turn of the century, fine 19th-century Oriental decorations, and dozens of four-foot flower bouquets can be found around every corner. No, this is not Princess Stephanie's West Coast abode; this is the home of musician and actress Courtney Love.

Courtney has a fantastic aesthetic sensibility. We have worked with her for many years on multiple homes, and her knowledge of the history of furniture and decorative arts is spectacular. We've shared our artistic journey, thoughts, and decorating ideas throughout each project. In working with Courtney, we have learned to appreciate the beauty in tattered fabrics and in the wear and weathering of an old chest or table. There's something fascinating about old things kept intact and aging gracefully without maintenance—it is like seeing into the past. It's deeply satisfying to work with a client at this level of participation, and the outcome of such collaboration is often sheer perfection.

previous pages
Mood boards for the Laurel Canyon project.

below, left
This chair was Kurt and Courtney's first furniture purchase when they "came into money."

below, right
Old English details like this black silk ottoman with red fringe tassels, mixed with new couture furnishings like the ravishing plum Emma Gardner rug represents Courtney's classic and chic sensibility.

opposite
Old and new exist together harmoniously in this Grand Ballroom, featuring furnishings by Majorelle, Sue et Mar, and Prelle, along with exquisite works of art from all over the world. The large-scale rug interacts beautifully with the smaller-scale patterns of the upholstered furniture.

following pages
The wall sconces flanking the door create a balanced arrangement that is echoed by the arrangement of furniture in this sitting room. Gold foil wallpaper with pink roses and lace lanterns by Sera of London create a romantic backdrop for exquisite Art Deco Sue et Mar lacquer chairs. The floral Prelle pattern and diamond-lattice patterns provide interesting contrast, while the matching blue tone brings it all together.

Prelle Fabric Mill has been weaving custom fabrics for more than 250 years and is the oldest silk-furnishing fabric factory in Lyon, France. The company has woven silk cloth for palaces and castles, such as Versailles and the Louvre. Today, clients can order identical reproductions of the company's earliest patterns, which makes Prelle a great resource for those who, like Courtney and us, enjoy bringing a bit of the past into their designs.

HISTORY'S MYSTERIES

Courtney collects the most enchanting and haunting curios, like antique porcelain dolls, old hand-painted pitchers from England (which she refers to as "piss pots"), century-old oil paintings of ghostlike silhouettes, crowns of thorns, and sacred-heart reliquaries. She has sentimental objets d'art collected over time from all over the world; she still has the chair she and late husband Kurt Cobain bought when they first came into money, as well as many gifts he gave her. All of these things are presented throughout the house, creating a fantastic sense of mystery, elegance, and wonder.

In many instances, concepts for brilliant spaces can be developed around just one incredible, unique piece. We designed the Red Room, inspired by an antique turn-of-the-century wallpaper pattern, as a guest bedroom for Courtney. She wanted a red boudoir reminiscent of an early 1900s Parisian brothel. We discovered the swatch of vintage wallpaper at Camden Passage, a flea market in London, and immediately were smitten by it! Wallpaper is the focal point of the room.

113

opposite

The landing of this stairway features a dramatic photograph of Courtney by Sam Taylor-Wood. Its enlarged size and use of light and shadow demand attention on the otherwise blank wall.

below, clockwise from top left

The Grand ballroom features age-old antiques and sumptuous textiles. These hand-painted doors in the Library are original to the house, from the 1920s. The library is notable for it's stenciled timber ceiling. Courtney's collections of romantic objects can be found throughout her home, giving each room an extra personal touch.

opposite

A headless mannequin that is more than one hundred years old sits perched on a French caned-back settee next to a baby grand piano. Curious antiques contribute to the overall artfulness of this home and reflect its owner's personality.

following pages

Courtney's beloved collection of antique porcelain dolls and intricate Baroque, miniature furniture. Antique figurines and heirlooms are displayed throughout the home, giving it a feeling of timelessness.

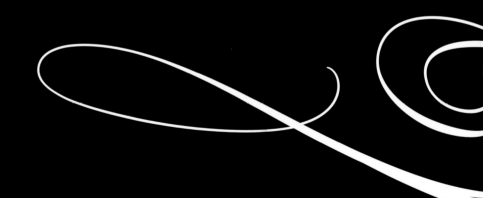

page 118

This rare chair inlaid with mother-of-pearl was a gift to Courtney from her husband, Kurt Cobain.

page 119, clockwise from top left

A bronze figure detail in a Sue et Mar cabinet; collection of curios and rock crystals; carved wood back of Majorelle chair.

opposite

This dramatic room of deep reds features a boudoir-style wallpaper and heart of thorns artwork.

above

A concept rendering of the boudoir and bedroom by Jaime Rummerfield.

Hollywood Style

Hollywood is a way of life in Los Angeles, not just a destination. The entertainment icons who live and work here dictate style in this town and around the world. When it comes to what's hot, Hollywood celebrities lead the way, whether it's clothing, jewelry, makeup, cars, or homes. For celebrities and other Angelenos, style is used to make a statement, and what people say with their living space tells you a lot about them. More than any other medium, your home is an expression of who you are and what your philosophy of life is—and in Hollywood, with the influence of a uniquely glamorous history and nearly unlimited resources, the forms that expression takes can be dazzling.

CHASEN ESTATE

Looking back on design history, there are a handful of designers who have most masterfully left a lasting impression. But, to us, the local icon that best epitomizes Hollywood style is architect Paul Williams.

Paul Williams' prolific career spanned a 50-year period, during which he helped define the "look" that Los Angeles retains to this day. He was the first noteworthy African American architect able to make a name for himself. His memorable style defined what we know today as Hollywood Regency and his amazing opulent designs, including his grand trademark balustrades and ornate staircases, have long inspired us in creating our own signature style, Modage. Known for impeccable taste and luscious California landscapes, Williams spent much of his career as architect to the stars, building homes for such notable celebrities as Tyrone Power, Barbara Stanwyck, Frank Sinatra, Lucille Ball and Desi Arnaz, and Zsa Zsa Gabor, to name just a few.

His design talents were not restricted to extravagant homes, either. Williams designed and redesigned other familiar Los Angeles landmarks, such as Perino's Restaurant, the Beverly Hills Hotel, the Beverly Wilshire Hotel, the Beverly Hills Saks Fifth Avenue, and the futuristic Theme Building in the middle of the Los Angeles Airport.

In 1953, Williams designed a magnificent mid-century home for Mr. and Mrs. Dave Chasen—for whom he also later redesigned the legendary Chasen's restaurant, a favorite celebrity haunt in Beverly Hills, now the location of Bristol Farms market on Beverly Boulevard and Doheny Drive. The former Chasen estate, now owned by our friends Beverly and Larry Schnur, sits on a two-acre plateau, high above Sunset Boulevard. A grand mid-century retreat with Regency flair, the Schnurs' historic home is a classic example of Hollywood style as it flourished during Hollywood's Golden Age of the 1950s and early '60s. Slowly cruising up the hill, you'll pass through the gates and find yourself transported to paradise.

The long driveway escorts you to an entry drive circling a cascading fountain. The grand back yard just begs you to relax while relishing the sweeping views of Los Angeles, and listening to Lionel Hampton's famous xylophone tunes chime in the distance; from here you can see clear from downtown to the ocean. Strolling the grounds, it's easy to be mesmerized by the dramatic views, from multiple vantage points, as the sun starts to set on the horizon. Trademark California palm trees and perfectly manicured pots of green-and-purple succulents frame a landscape adorned with Richard Schultz outdoor furniture and authentic 1960s pieces that have survived decades of summers. Oh, if those pieces could talk! This is an entertainer's home, a California destination home at its finest. Just sitting out here with Beverly by the pool, as we love to do, invites us to imagine the laughter rolling through star-studded outdoor parties, where the biggest Hollywood players would chat it up over bowls of Chasen's famous chili.

The house is simply extraordinary. Its grand, large-scale rooms—another Paul Williams signature—and incredible views of the city are an ideal setting for enjoying life. The provenance of the house and its tangible links to the past give a sense of history and Hollywood style that inspires us anew every time we visit.

previous pages, left
The Hollywood set of The Women, *starring Joan Crawford, inspired our concept for the Versace Room in the* Esquire *Showcase House.*

previous pages, right
Woodson and Rummerfield's Cherry Blossom Print was created for singer Christina Aguilera.

Below, left to right
Outdoor meals are a staple of Hollywood style. Beverly, Ron, Jaime, and Patrick have lunch poolside while taking in the view of Los Angeles; A simple black and white table setting makes for an elegant backdrop to colorful fruit and tea treats on vintage service dishes; luxurious cars, classic stone driveways, grand fountains, and palm trees are a frequently observed combination in front of Hollywood estates.

opposite
It's easy to imagine the Chasen estate's grand back yard populated by Hollywood's biggest stars, as it was during the 1950s and '60s.

GRAND STYLE

We first worked with Versace on the *Esquire* magazine showcase house, a project in Beverly Ridge Terrace that was a fantastic example of high style and expression within a space. We were given a large part of the estate to design using couture Versace furniture, which we mixed with worldly antiques and unique finds. The resulting Great Room and bar area have "sophisticated living" written all over them. But the loggia really speaks to us as a classic Hollywood setting.

The house *Esquire* used for this showcase is perched high above the city. The Great Room opens up to a majestic 360-degree view that we just had to take advantage of with a fabulously outfitted outdoor loggia. The loggia invites you to enjoy the trademark California ocean breezes and misty sunshine, and it beckons for a luxurious afternoon nap. And as the sun sets and the interior lights dim in the bar, the first cocktail—a staple of Hollywood style—is served. A Manhattan, anyone?

An important accessory for outdoor living, hanging fabrics can be closed to provide shade or to create a buffer from a light tropical rain. Our loggia is surrounded by panels of two-tone linen, white tops with black bottoms, and tied back with gold-braided tassels that add a touch of old-world glamour. The breezy fabric brings softness to the area and makes it feel more intimate. We divided the room into two distinct conversation areas—perfect for rubbing elbows—using black indoor/outdoor carpet pieces cut into rectangles; the knotted pile of the rugs creates tactile interest against the smooth Jerusalem travertine stone floors and also helps anchor the furniture.

One conversation area utilizes a sectional sofa, while the other consists of a collection of chairs and settees. All the Versace pieces are made of tailored, basket-weave frames,

which up the natural texture factor; chicness is maintained with a definitive black finish. The chairs feature a predominantly black, outdoor fabric printed with large white roses—the scale of which stands out against the couch and settee fabric, a more evenly black-and-white acanthus-leaf pattern. To further blur the lines between indoor and outdoor, we added some decorative landscaping: These petrified manzanita trees add the perfect element of surprise. Glass hurricanes with candles in them create a sunset glow throughout the loggia, setting the stage for an evening of cocktails and hobnobbing or making the loggia an elegant launching pad for a night on the town.

previous pages
We admire the colorful and tailored living room of the Chasen estate designed by Neil Korpinen and Rick Erickson.

opposite, top
In the Esquire Showcase House project, indoor/outdoor living is facilitated by the smooth transition between the Versace-appointed Great Room and the plush loggia. A common color scheme helps tie it all together.

opposite, bottom
A luxurious outdoor room showcasing Versace's outdoor furniture collection.

below
A part of our Road Map for this project: a perspective sketch of the Great Room and a furniture layout for the Great Room and loggia.

following pages
Ron and Jaime on the bar in the Great Room at the Esquire Showcase House. The deep red griffins on the wallpaper create a powerful background for the primarily black and white color scheme of the bar. Tall, ornate white urns are in wonderful proportion to and contrast dramatically with clusters of smaller, simpler black noir crystal decanters. We love how the griffin pattern references European nobility, as if to say, "This is today's castle."

pages 132-133
The Esquire Showcase House Great Room features furniture from the Versace Home collection, table lamps from Therien & Co., and both new and old decoratives from Woodson and Rummerfield's House of Design.

129

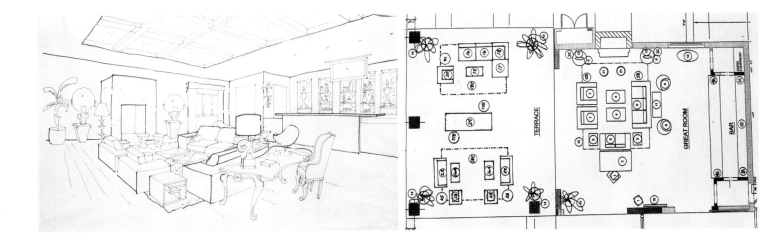

Hollywood is all about the glitzy details, and Hollywood homes are no exception. We collected nearly twenty black noir and clear crystal decanters, both vintage and new, to mix with candelabras all in one cluster on an up-lit console table. The decanters are of a similar shape but provide high contrast in color for impact. The quantity of the collection makes a striking visual statement.

JEWELRY FOR THE HOME

Several charity events were held against the backdrop we created at the *Esquire* showcase, and because the design of the rooms was such a hit with guests, we were asked to collaborate with Versace again on yet another extraordinary event: the Walk of Style, an event commemorating the ten-year anniversary of Gianni Versace's passing and honoring Donatella Versace for her achievements leading the company since then. We were fortunate to collaborate again with Alan Rohwer in developing a swanky concept for this A-list, spotlight-worthy event.

The Walk of Style was hosted in a large tented structure, erected on the Beverly Hills City Hall lawn. Everyone from film producers to supermodels to actors came out to celebrate all that is Versace—dressed in Versace clothing, of course. We even ran into some of our favorite clients! The entrance to the event, a driveway stretching between two sections of the lawn, became the "red carpet," where valets waited to take guests' cars. Flanked by two fifteen-foot-tall, gold-leafed Art Deco angels, the scene harkened back to a glamorous Old Hollywood Oscars night. The long walkway

opened up into the tent foyer, where guests were greeted by a decadent supper-club-meets-21st-century-chic affair.

The walls of the tent were upholstered with a bold, wide-striped black-and-white indoor/outdoor fabric and lit from above by stunning overscaled brass Deco chandeliers. The huge size of the light fixtures was in perfect proportion to the extra-high ceilings of the tents—anything smaller would have disappeared against the cavernous backdrop.

Food and bar displays made space for guests to congregate and share their favorite Versace memories, and a custom Lamborghini, with a Versace-designed interior (featuring the Greek key pattern), which was to be auctioned off later in the evening, was on display.

The main room featured a tiered seating area arranged around a stage, with a special VIP-seating section closest to the stage itself. We used the same Versace furniture from the *Esquire* showcase to outfit the VIP section, making it a mansion-worthy living space for the high-profile guests. The

Famous Los Angeles supper clubs like Ciro's epitomized high-style dining in the early to mid-1900s. Soft mood lighting lent fantastic sparkle to gowns and jewelry; luxe fabrics covered cushions and walls, often draping in corners to provide privacy for the highest profile diners. We wanted the Walk of Style event to give guests a similar experience of luxurious exclusivity.

HISTORY'S MYSTERIES

majority of the tables were arranged on the main floor and also on a riser along the outer walls (in the 1920s and '30s, supper clubs commonly had different levels in the main dining room, and we wanted to recreate that experience for the guests). We mostly stuck to a white-on-white color palette to ensure that the decorations wouldn't compete with the Versace pieces—fashions and furniture alike—on display. The tables were dressed simply with white tablecloths and silver Chevalier chairs. We added battery-operated candelabras with shades to each table to keep the light soft and the room glowing. Beautiful cascading flower arrangements in vintage urns—a classic Italian look—placed throughout the tent brought in pockets of natural color and helped to keep the dramatic color scheme from being too severe, as did an abundance of plush cushions and draped fabric.

The event was spectacular. We watched reels from 1980s fashion shows with supermodels such as Cindy, Naomi, and Christy strutting down the runway in Gianni Versace's captivating ensembles—and enjoyed seeing these same women sitting front and center, enjoying the memories. Elton John

performed, as did Guns N' Roses. The space was divine; elegant, chic, and comfortable, it was the perfect vessel for an elite evening. But in a flash, it was dismantled and gone, with no trace to be found by morning. Just another night in Hollywood.

previous pages
This view from the back yard looking into the decadent loggia and Great Room at twilight is stunning—worthy of the Hollywood elite who congregated here.

below
Jaime, Ron, and Alan Rohwer from Versace share a jovial moment at Woodson and Rummerfield's House of Design.

OLD-WORLD CHIC

When it comes to A-list residences, we've had the opportunity to spend time with some really fantastic people. Actress Kelly Preston is one of them. She's such a blast to work with—she has a great design sensibility and a love for beautiful things. She's also hilarious, keeping us in stitches throughout our meetings with her. But when it's time to get down to business, she knows what she wants.

We recently assisted Kelly and husband, John Travolta, in designing a kitchen renovation for their California Spanish home. The kitchen was tired but spacious, reminiscent of a 1950s Spanish-style, but with 1970s dark woods and add-on detailing that needed to go. After a series of discussions, we established the design concept: "old-world chic," not too old, not too contemporary (think 19th-century European with some modern elements, but nothing hypermodern). This was quite fitting and complementary to the house and its existing décor, which is very laid back yet exquisite and tasteful, with lots of tranquil color schemes, rich patterns, and elegant, comfortable furniture.

As Kelly requested, we did a lot of tone-on-tone work with subtle accents in this room. The novel colorway incorporates a fresh, crisp paint combination of a light, buttery yellow, called Ivoire, and a dreamy green, called Sea Salt. We painted the cabinets white and used glass fronts that allow you to see inside, which we finished in another shade of green. The magnificent island, slightly overscaled but in perfect proportion to the rest of the large room, features a gray-green and white granite top, honed to a smooth matte finish instead of the more common glossy sheen.

opposite

Designing is so creative, and so much fun! We love clients who want to be fully engaged in the process. Here we are with Kelly and her assistant Tracee Falkow (left) reviewing mood boards for John and Kelly's new kitchen.

below

Tracee, Jaime, Kelly, and Ron finalizing the kitchen design.

The new floors are farmhouse-style, with wide planking in a warm honey tone with a tung oil finish. Kelly had the fantastic idea of putting in an old cottage fireplace with a wood mantel, which brought warmth to the room and tied together the wood floors and timber ceilings. It really added a wow factor to the space. And because Kelly's family likes to hang out in the kitchen, we built in a soft, plush breakfast nook big enough to seat many friends and family members. She selected a wonderful patterned fabric in green and yellow tones for the custom brasserie-style banquette; the large-scale print helps draw your eye to the area. To give it all a stylish finish, the banquette and surrounding old pie screen–style cabinets were painted in contrasting black high-gloss paint. Accessories such as cooking herbs under glass cloches and antique decorations such as vintage crockery add beauty and comfort.

This house was built during the 1950s boom, when architects designed whole neighborhoods of large, sprawling homes, which only Hollywood celebrities could afford. This era celebrated the work of the famous California tile-makers, particularly in Spanish-style homes like Kelly and John's. Bathrooms and kitchens frequently featured very distinctive handmade tile-work. The house's heritage was too good to ignore, so we decided to take the kitchen back to its former glory days by adding beautiful tile accents.

An original archway niche on one wall had previously been painted over, causing it to fade into the wall. We accented its architectural integrity by creating a backsplash of Ann Sacks 8-by-8-inch Moroccan-style Arabesque tiles in a delicious pistachio color. Because the island is the first thing you see when you enter the kitchen, we decided to really capture

the eye by creating tiled fronts for its cabinetry; these 6-by-6-inch tiles, called Kasbah, are in a vibrant, green-and-white woven pattern that is complementary to the negative space of the pattern of the Arabesque tiles in the archway. The different style of tiles in the same matte pistachio–and-white color scheme adds a wonderful textural layer and visual language to the kitchen, bringing variety to the vertical finishes, complementing the paint tones, and interacting harmoniously with the white cabinets. People tend to forget about tile until the last minute, but taking the time to plan and mix things up with a variety of beautiful patterns brings movement and life to the room.

The space turned out to be a warm, welcoming space for Kelly and her family to enjoy, but we knew it needed something extra special to give it that Hollywood sparkle. To add

some glamour, we suspended three birdcage-style chandeliers with an antiqued-mirror finish above the island. The kitchen is worthy of any star-studded meal! With a little updating, manicuring, and styling, the room became sensational—a perfect fit for its classy, and chic owners.

opposite and above

Mood boards with fabric samples, color fan-deck selections, and inspiration imagery helped us translate Kelly's vision.

following pages, left

The completed kitchen is a clean combination of classic and chic. The Bagues sconces from France, made of mercury glass and crystal, contrast with the rustic wooden countertop.

following pages, clockwise from top

A cheerful palette of sea salt green and Ivoire yellow make the fireplace seating area welcoming. The powder room, like the kitchen, contrasts warm woods with elegant, jewel-like accessories. Natural light floods the kitchen.

Mining for Gold

One of the biggest and best parts of our process involves hunting for those treasures that will make a statement or perfectly accent a design theme we're working with. That means going shopping! We travel all over the country and various parts of the world mining for gold, a key element of our Modage philosophy. We never know where we'll find that perfect little something—it could be a signature Sasha Brastoff ashtray or a Giò Ponti cocktail table—and studying the histories of furniture, art, and architecture comes in handy. Our knowledge of design history helps us spot a classic Nakashima daybed or recognize the Charles Field Haviland china "lifesaver" mark. But you don't need to go back to school—even watching television programs like "Antiques Roadshow" helps sharpen the eye on the hunt. When we travel, we look for noteworthy furnishings, signed and pedigreed art, and other decorative objects. But above all, a piece has to "smile" at or "speak" to us in order to make it into our shopping tote! Our favorite spots are off the beaten path in charming little towns, where we've met some of the most interesting, knowledgeable people and forged lasting artistic relationships.

HOW TO SHOP

We've found incredible gems in some very surprising places. We've traveled all over Europe, browsed boutique shops in America's biggest cities, and spent hours digging through tables of miscellaneous objects at garage sales, flea markets, and antique stores in tiny, forgotten towns. Treasures can be anywhere, waiting for you to discover them.

Once something has won your attention, inspect it thoroughly. Look for markings that might reference its provenance, such as a signature, crest, or dates, and make sure the piece is not damaged or flawed. But don't let a few scratches or a nick stop you from taking home a great find—imperfection isn't always a bad thing, especially with vintage items. To us, it's character.

By no means should you second-guess your decision to purchase something that grabs you. More often than not there's someone behind you ready to snatch it up. We've had this happen to us too many times. Once we were shopping in a small Pennsylvania town and fell in love with an old Adirondack rocking chair made of sticks and twigs. We thought it would be an interesting twist for a very modern room. We decided to keep looking and come back to it

when we were finished, but a handsomely dressed pair of gentlemen spied the piece and purchased it right out from under our noses. If something speaks to you, no matter how small it is, the best thing to do is have the shopkeeper put it on hold while you continue to browse and ponder. When you see an item that brings you joy and you fall head over heels for it, get it. Seeing that very special piece in your home or work space will enrich your everyday life for years to come.

previous pages, left
Antique shops are a treasure trove of decorative delights.

previous pages, right
"Roman Soldiers" pattern by florence broadhurst.

opposite
One of our favorite pastimes is perusing art collections for that perfect piece.

following pages, left
Ron and Jaime taking a break while shopping for clients.

following pages, right
John Connell showing us some fantastic trinkets in his Palm Springs shop.

We found two pairs of the exact same chair within one year, at different, small furniture shops in L.A. The size and shape make them an ideal showcase for two-toned fabrics. The high, wide backs also provide a great opportunity to make a statement, so we used a large-scale faux zebra pattern on one set of the chairs and a dynamic contrast of faux black-crocodile skin and white vinyl on the other. These types of regal chairs are perfect for mixing up dining-room-table seating—place them at the heads of the table.

JEWELRY FOR THE HOME

WHAT TO DO WITH YOUR FINDS

Now that you've purchased that perfect piece on your treasure hunt, you may find that it needs a little dressing up. When redoing furniture, there are a few things to keep in mind. First, if you start with the most luxurious items, the essentials will take care of themselves. You can give old furniture a really polished look if you refinish in high-gloss paint. We prefer black or white. For re-upholstering, always start with the best fabric you can afford, because the fabric is what people will have the most interaction with—first visually, then through touch. Higher–quality fabrics feel better, and they last longer, too. Furniture with high or wide expanses looks great with bold, contrasting colors or large prints. If you're thinking about button tufting, use solid colors. If you button-tuft a large printed fabric, you'll lose the pattern. Add accents like you do with fashion. When tying together the ensemble, it is important to pay attention to details—embellishments like nail heads, fringe trims, cording/piping, and tassels complete a piece and add a tailored finish.

The best way to find a good upholsterer is word of mouth. Ask around, and at the very least ask for and call references given by potential choices. Working with antiques is a specialty, and the best craftsmen will be able to show you that they have experience in this area. Refinishing and painting are usually done by the same people who work on reupholstering, but intricate work may require the skills of a specialized refinisher (for example, lacquering is a more complicated process than applying high-gloss paint). The key to getting what you want is to provide a paint chip or to ask for samples from the shop to approve. Any high-end antique gallery should be able to recommend someone, and they often offer these services in-house when you purchase a piece from their selection. When you get into very high-end antiques, however, you actually don't want to mess with them—these are more valuable in their original state.

opposite

A slipper chair by Woodson and Rummerfield's upholstered in Cranes by Florence Broadhurst.

below

Florence Broadhurst fabric samples exemplify how patterns in different scales but similar color schemes can work together beautifully. From left to right, Circles and Squares, Cranes, and Japanese Bamboo.

following pages

We unearthed this late-1950s gem of a sofa at an estate sale in La Jolla, California. The lines on the sofa are very stylized—from a scrolled arm and button detail to the two-cushion seat and four-cushion back. Originally covered in a solid silk, we kept the details but reupholstered in a bold canary yellow and white pattern called Circles and Squares, which is more vibrant and graphic. We displayed the revised version of this sofa on our showroom floor for only five days before one of L.A.'s A-list ladies came in and snatched it up—we knew we had a winner.

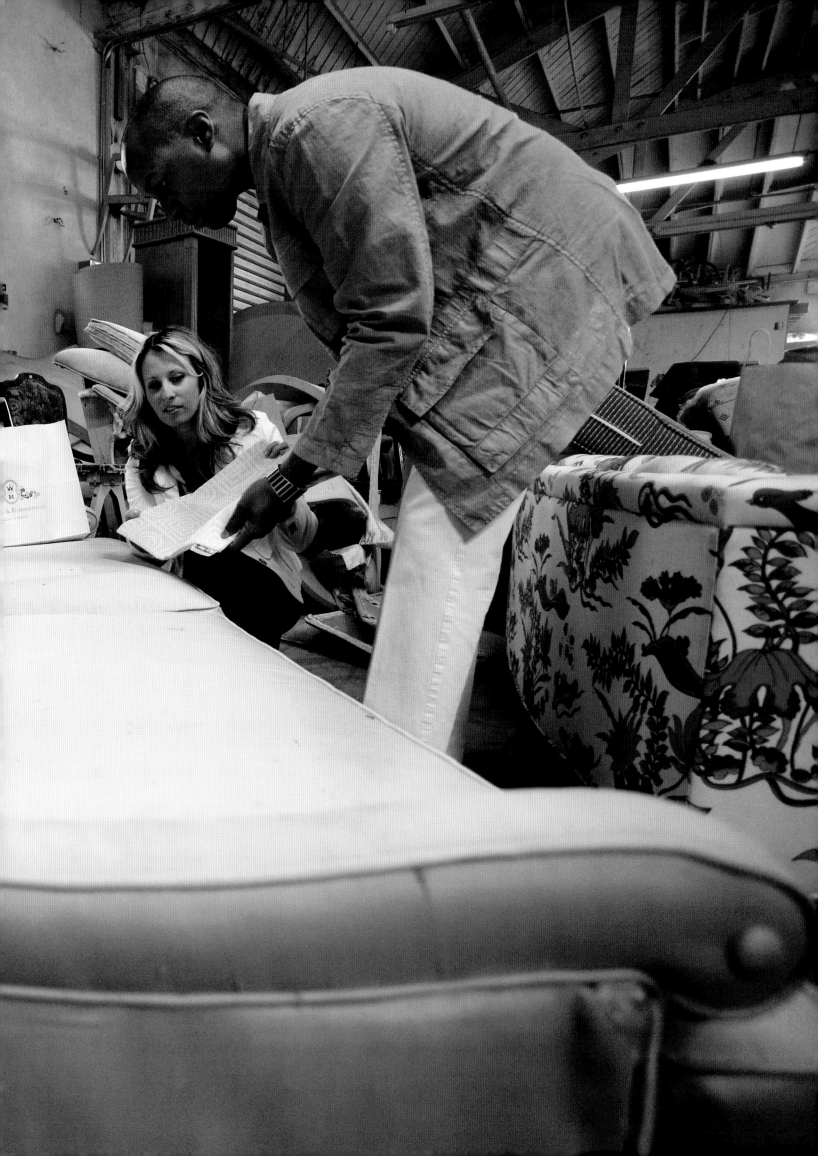

Though large pieces like furniture make grand statements, remember to accessorize. Oftentimes, the interaction between smaller objects and larger ones can finish the look of a room. A colorful piece of artwork can pull together the different tones in furniture or decorations throughout the space. A standout glass object looks sleek next to a velvet chair or in front of a backdrop of highly tactile drapes. Objets d'art and decorative art make great conversation pieces and leave a lasting impression on your guests. Whether you showcase them on your mantel or on shelves throughout your home, you can achieve a pulled-together, curated feel for your glassware and ceramic collectibles by shopping for objects with the same colors or by creating a family of similar-type objects.

Major finds can dazzle and bring a whole room together. On a trip to Italy, for example, we were strolling through the piazzas in Venice and came across a student art show. From a distance, we spotted this amazingly large drawing of a shouting boy's face and instantly knew we had to have it. The artist was nineteen years old! We found someone who could translate for us and had a wonderfully engaging discussion about purchasing his work. He later introduced us to his father, who was thrilled beyond belief that Americans—from Los Angeles, no less—wanted to purchase his son's art. We settled on a price and happily sealed the deal. The entire experience was very special and memorable.

opposite

This end of the living room is outfitted with redone vintage Milo Baughman, Harry Bertoia, and Eames chairs. Interesting objets d'art and large-scale artwork by student Guglielmo Alfawir add warm personality and memories to the chic array. The other artwork is by Steven Walters.

right, top

African art displayed against white walls and modern, mirrored surfaces add texture, contrast, and surprising personality to a room.

155

We discovered these uniquely shaped end tables at a furniture liquidation company in East Los Angeles. The tables were destined for a moody, sexy bedroom, the focal point of which was a custom bed, made of vinyl and Lucite. The crocodile complements the shiny surface of the bed while also adding another layer of texture.

JOURNEY OF AN OBJECT

We decided to make this piece the focal point of a client's living room. The strong, rough lines of charcoal, depicting a boy's intense facial expression, conveyed so much emotion. It jars the room, giving us the texture and depth we needed to balance the soft white, blue, and green tones in this otherwise tranquil space. The drawing is also very gritty and almost unfinished looking—the perfect counter to our streamlined, polished furniture and mod glass decorations.

opposite

Rare finds such as these vintage plates by Rosenthal, commemorating the establishment of the original thirteen U.S. colonies, make an impact when arranged as a group, such as in this display in the House of Design showroom.

following pages

This living room is Modage at its finest, with its glamorous 21st-century mixture of old and new. The cool, serene color palette is accented by the smooth crystal and mirrored surfaces of Woodson & Rummerfield's Ambassador mirrors and Wilshire console tables, Barcelona coffee table, and Milo Baughman chairs. The simple, clean lines of the Metropolitan sofa and other furniture pieces contrast with the ornate mirrors, candelabra, and sunburst hanging mirror. A zebra-print rug draws the eye to the center and adds interest to the mix of subtle patterns found throughout the room.

BRINGING IT ALL TOGETHER

Once we acquire our fabulous finds, we haul them back to our boutique in Los Angeles. Some objects need only to be cleaned and labeled with a price tag, while others need significantly more work. We find it fascinating to refinish, refurbish, and breathe new life into a piece; we call on skilled professionals to turn our visions into reality. Some of our "born again" pieces are immediately incorporated into our showroom décor and offered for sale, and others are earmarked for clients' homes. Sometimes, when we are inspired by a certain piece, we create a whole room around it. Our showroom floor naturally evolves over time through the introduction of spectacularly inspiring finds.

For example, our entire Winter Wonderland showroom installation was inspired by two vintage sweetheart chairs, named the Beverlywood Chairs, which we reupholstered in a very contemporary turquoise, with white accents for stark contrast. On the walls, we used a stunning silver-foiled Spanish lace–patterned wallpaper inside the Regency-style reveals (wood trim molded into framelike shapes), and turquoise paint on the rest of the walls to highlight the architectural details of the room—incorporating just enough of the brazen color and metallic detail to be complementary,

not overpowering. We also used a few punches of turquoise accents throughout the room to provide balance. The Harlow-sofa upholstery features silk with a trellis pattern in ice blue—a lighter hue than the turquoise—and the nubby, large-scale pattern rug anchors the seating arrangement. The rug—along with the portrait and formally decorated mantel—also balances the expansiveness of the high, smooth walls by bringing the eye back to the center as it grounds the room. At the center of it all, the Socialite portrait over the mantel ties the room together with its silvery frame, blue background, and the subject's gentle but sophisticated 1950s style.

opposite

The Lord and Lady of high style in our showroom with Versace Couture chairs and our own Chrysanthemum wallpaper and black Ambassador mirror.

following pages

Our Winter Wonderland installation at Woodson and Rummerfield's House of Design illustrates the use of patterns and one bold accent color—turquoise, in this case—to highlight the architectural details of a room and to add an element of glamorous fun. Beverlywood sofa and chairs, both by Woodson and Rummerfield's foiled wallpaper shines by the light of the Moooi Shade Chandeliers. A fabulous vintage find, our "Socialite" painting, presides over all in its place above the mantle.

We came across this "Socialite" painting in a New Jersey antique shop where the owners resided in a room at the end of the stairway; the painting caught our eye through the many layers of artwork strewn along the store walls. We admired her satin gown and magnificent diamond ring and were struck by her surprisingly kind, blue eyes—but the existing dark, heavy frame didn't do her justice. We replaced it with a more elegant, hand-carved, silver-leafed French frame. The bright metallic finish and simple curves of our frame lightened the painting and gave its classic subject new life.

JOURNEY OF AN OBJECT

To accessorize the room a bit, we featured a whimsical Raymond Loewy birdcage tea set that we unearthed in a little antique store in coastal Ventura, California. We were thrilled to find the complete set in mint condition, hiding in a dusty display cabinet.

JEWELRY FOR THE HOME

opposite, top

This Menswear showroom installation is decked out in an elegant yet decidedly masculine fashion. Low on frills but high on style, subtle textures and colors such as the charcoal velvet of the kidney-shaped sofa and understated patterns like the geometric key print on the reclaimed wingback chairs keep the room moody and classy.

following pages

Elkins chairs compliment the forms and color pop of an Angela Adams rug in the breakfast nook; The beachy kitchen is fresh and chic yet still pay's homage to it's 1920's roots; "Japanese Floral" a vivid pattern by Florence Broadhurst lines the insets of the dining room sideboard cabinet.

We also did a Menswear showroom installation, inspired by a vintage fashion palette from men's suits and a 1930s mannequin head originally from a New York City department store. The debonair and warm palette of gray and parchment ivory (like a suit and starched shirt) is offset by bright, colorful accents, like the pair of 1950s green-and-yellow ceramic birds and 1930s Nubian-style, or "blackamoor," lamps. Outlawed at one time because they depicted black slaves, these lamps are now collectors' items. A hefty, masculine oil painting anchors the fireplace.

The two wingback chairs are covered in a small-scale reek key fabric—a perfect contrast in proportion to the large kidney-shaped 1950s sofa that fills one side of the room. The delicate 1940s reverse-mirror painted-glass coffee table, believed to be from Cuba, offers a tactile surprise with its smooth surface and braided-rope edging, which has flaked away over the years to expose a wonderful array of gilded layers.

So California, So Modage

This client's home is nestled where the city meets the sea in Santa Monica—a sanctuary where beauty flourishes, style is abundant, and the nostalgia of starlet opulence hangs on the air. Mix in some California charm, top it off with a dash of international flavor, and you have the perfect setting for this enchanted 1920s bungalow. Our client, Kendall Rhodes, is a dedicated film buff and producer, and it was important that her house represent this passion. This is a woman who reads thirty scripts a week! So to honor the bungalow as her private cocoon, we set out to make the place over as a "Modage-film cocktail." Imagine a drop of young Jack Nicholson, a splash of Eva Gabor and Anne Bancroft, finished with a Stanley Kubrick twist. To capture this essence, we went on the hunt for mod-style details and fresh finishes to mix with daring-yet-tranquil color. Now, this little bungalow is anything but demure.

We used a brash color palette, heavy on the greens and blues, inspired by the home's proximity to the sea, but kept it more saturated than the typical beach house, morphing tones from one room to another. The furniture and artwork that we chose reflect European mod forms from the '60s, but we also included some hypermodern items like a Marc Newson coffee table and a chinois breakfast table by IGE to reflect our client's upbeat freshness and desire for style.

opposite

A modern chandelier with a vintage twist.

below

The IGE table with an inlaid wood chrysanthemum is a perfect example of using scale to emphasize an image. The flower pattern complements the quirky and colorful Angela Adams custom rug; the circular table shape is repeated by the Frances Elkin chair backs.

following pages

The breakfast area features classic Frances Elkin chairs covered in modern kelly green vinyl fabric. The 1940s green Italian decanter set made of hand-blown glass is in mint condition; we found it at a gallery café, set up in a converted barn, on our way to the airport in New Jersey. The unique Trojan-horse textile on the wall has a wonderful raised, soft texture and brilliant colors. We came across it at an old ranch estate sale in Oceanside, California, and thought it was perfectly evocative of the crafty 1960s; the hand-carved frame makes it more sophisticated than kitsch.

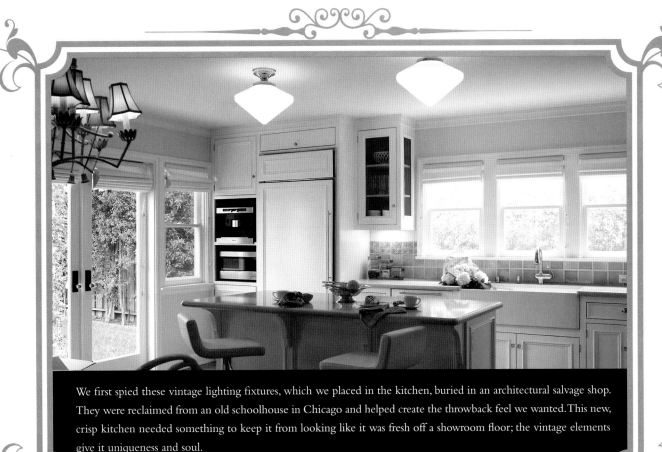

We first spied these vintage lighting fixtures, which we placed in the kitchen, buried in an architectural salvage shop. They were reclaimed from an old schoolhouse in Chicago and helped create the throwback feel we wanted. This new, crisp kitchen needed something to keep it from looking like it was fresh off a showroom floor; the vintage elements give it uniqueness and soul.

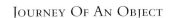

JOURNEY OF AN OBJECT

Los Angeles homes from the early to mid-twentieth century are known for a certain style of curios and tchotchkes, most notably kitschy ceramic animals: Birds of all types were the most popular. Also common were oversized keys and metal floral sculptures hung on walls, and big marble or glass grape bunches gracing tabletops in bowls or on their own. We enjoy bringing items like these into projects as a hallmark of our style and influence—they're a reminder of what once was. There is something wonderful about this. Decorative objects are a symbol of the times, evoking memories of a bygone era: Haven't you heard someone say, "Oh my mother had one of these when I was growing up"? This updated interior stays true to form with a trio of hens, purchased from three separate vintage stores, perched on the dining table; a life-size porcelain whippet, acquired from a celebrity estate sale, guarding the master bedroom; and "good luck" gazelle busts adorns the fireplace mantel. (War-era homes of the 1930s and '40s often displayed small gazelles and deer as signs of good luck.) The gazelle busts here are a new version, made to look old. We love that these busts are larger in scale, which makes a statement—in the '30s, they would have been half the size.

While we considered hitting some antique shops and dealers for vintage artwork, Kendall already had a great collection of photographs and paintings, specifically portraits of her mother and aunt from the 1960s. They looked like models! We love portraits, especially California stylized portraits from the '60s, distinctive for their magical, almost Disneyesque feel. Subjects are typically shown from the side, wearing smiles on upturned, sun-kissed faces, with hair and makeup that are almost too perfect to be real. They can set the tone of an entire room and are another signature of our work. These were just what we needed to round out the overall design concept and they made the home that much more personal.

opposite
Kitchen cabinets with glass fronts and painted insets add interest, while the button floral tile complements the painted shelves.

173

Asian figurines and artwork in the living and dining rooms greet visitors to the house. These were purchased from a one-armed lady named Jenny who is an expert in Asian imports from the 1920s, '30s, and '40s. Jenny is smart as a whip and knows her stuff. She is an excellent resource for these relics and has a whimsical story to tell about every piece. In her younger years, when international shipping was no easy feat, Jenny traveled to various Asian countries and collected a multitude of items. Most of them ended up housed in a storage facility in California and are still sitting there, five decades later—it's a mysterious treasure trove of art. We described what we wanted, and Jenny promised us she had something perfect. When we returned to the shop, she presented us with this adorable artifacts such as this one. These items, with their vivid colors and fun, exotic look, add personality to the rooms.

JOURNEY OF AN OBJECT

opposite

The guest bedroom featuring Woodson & Rummerfield's Chrysanthemum wallpaper is bright and airy—perfect for a beachside abode in Santa Monica. Pretty floral details in red echo the pattern of the wallpaper on a smaller scale.

left

A fashion photo of Kendall's mother and aunt in the late '60s adorns a wall in the guest bedroom.

following pages, left

A white ceramic gazelle bust is for good luck. It also finishes a great-looking display arranged next to smaller colored vases with gold accents.

following pages, right

Vintage Asian figurine in all shades of green. A little gold provides some sparkle.

The South Pacific–style, handmade, Capiz-shell globes, imported from Argentina, are an exquisite accessory in the master bathroom. Their unexpected yet tasteful presence makes this room extra special, and the shells remind the elegant room of its beach-house roots.

JOURNEY OF AN OBJECT

Kendall didn't want to enlarge the original footprint of the house, but an expansion was definitely in order, so we decided to add a master suite, media room, and a rooftop sundeck. For the master bedroom, we outfitted the space with a French-style carved bed, painted antique white, and a fireplace facade with Art Nouveau details, imported from London. The bed itself is a celebration of textures and patterns, with its ensemble of raised and smooth velvets and quilted silks in shades of pink, gold, and chocolate brown. The table lamps are vintage 1970s, purchased at an antiques mall in Palm Springs. The lamps perfectly complemented our mix of heirlooms, updated and arranged with a modern sensibility. The custom nightstands, inspired by 1950s and '60s boudoir dressing tables, and which we reinvented by combining the mirror drawer fronts with a wooden frame and tabletop, help give this shared bedroom a nice balance of feminine and masculine.

We're always emphasizing to people the joys of mining for gold and incorporating these finds into their everyday lives. It's important to pay attention to what feels right and not get too hung up on being matchy-matchy or sticking to one absolute style. Our philosophy of high style is about finding the perfect piece that will work with all your other favorite objects; that piece doesn't always have to be expensive — it might be a sweet little vase you find in a dusty roadside antique shop. The number of things you can resurrect from the past and make new again is limitless. The hunt is a real thrill, but you must give yourself permission to acquire what speaks to you. The result is a home that reflects who you are and even where you've been. That is the real treasure.

opposite, top

A dreamy beach bungalow living room infused with green and blue tones inspired by the sea.

opposite, bottom left

A vintage Murano glass bowl reflects the beachy color palette for the bungalow.

opposite, bottom right

This mirrored vanity on large-scale black and white hexagon tile creates a dynamic contrast.

following pages

This sumptuous master suite balances the femininity of pink with French Roast walls and sophisticated striped lampshades. Modern His & Hers mirrored end tables add an unexpected twist beside the bed's collection of decadent velvet and silk textures.

California Dreamin'

Los Angeles has the distinction of being one of the only major cities in the United States where you can enjoy the outdoors practically all year round. Even in the middle of December, you can experience some of the most vibrant sunsets from your back deck, or as you're strolling along the beach with little more than a light sweater. Angelenos enjoy a true indoor/outdoor lifestyle, courtesy of the glorious weather; sunshine, convertible cars, pools, and palm trees abound.

On any given day, you can take Sunset Boulevard west all the way to the ocean, and you'll find surfers and sun worshipers soaking up the rays. All too often, you can find us tooling around in a vintage roadster, top down, with a small chair or table tucked in the back from one of our shopping excursions. But it's the magic hour—the strikingly beautiful evening—that brings out our inner entertainers, motivating us to create outdoor dinner parties and social gatherings.

California sunsets are legendary. The unbelievably gorgeous array of oranges, yellows, ambers, and pinks are the hallmarks of our evenings, just like the *Endless Summer* surf-movie poster that inspires us with the mood it evokes. There are a host of lookout points around the city that allow visitors to fully enjoy the perfect vistas, such as the hike up to the Hollywood sign, several trails in the Santa Monica mountains, a hike through Runyon Canyon in the Hollywood Hills, Griffith Observatory in Griffith Park, and of course, any number of beaches along the coast. Many times, though, it's the view from your own home that feels just right.

previous pages, left
Southern California's trademark golden sunset.

previous pages, right
"Paris" pattern by Florence Broadhurst

below
Jaime and Ron enjoying "good vibrations" on the sands of Santa Monica.

opposite
You can find inspiration most everywhere you look, such as in this incredible large-scale graphic street art along La Brea Avenue.

following pages
Jaime soaking up some afternoon rays on the balcony of our Micheltorena Street project in Silver Lake.

Entertaining in the Magic Hour

Enjoyment of sunsets and ocean breezes is maximized out-doors, so it's no wonder that outdoor entertaining is such a huge part of California living. The temperate weather allows for wonderful barbecues at the beach and picnics in the park, as well as delightful social gatherings in the back yard around the pool, especially in the long summer months. An evening backyard soiree is a wonderful opportunity to play with style in a temporary setting while spending time with favorite friends and family. We believe this is what a lush life is all about.

One of our clients' homes, on Micheltorena Street, nestled in the Silver Lake Hills east of Hollywood and northwest of downtown Los Angeles, has a wonderful setting for a festive outdoor affair. The architecture of Silver Lake developed with the growing film industry in the early 1900s; Silver Lake and adjacent Edendale and Echo Park were home to many early motion-picture studios. Silver Lake has been home to many filmmakers, actors, and directors, such as Gloria Swanson, Stan Laurel, Oliver Hardy, Antonio Moreno, and many others. Moreno, a silent-era film star, became the well-known developer behind many neighborhoods in the region, most of which were modeled after Mediterranean villages he visited. This house was built in 1953 and illustrates a subtle transition from the stucco and arches that were very popular in the 1930s and '40s to the more modern lines and materials of the 1950s. Both the front and back walls of the home are made of glass, which blurs the barrier between indoors and outdoors.

The backyard setting of the home is naturally romantic and tranquil, a perfect little oasis in the city. We lined the perimeter of the yard with torches to add a little drama and strategically placed candles to saturate the yard with ambient lighting. The green color palette was inspired by the abundant foliage in the landscape, and we added accents of gold to reflect the light of the torches, which created a magical, sparkling effect. The pool is a perfect backdrop—we tied it into the scheme by adding splashes of bright turquoise on the table and throughout the three-tiered patio.

below, left

The Silver Lake reservoir, nestled between the hills east of Hollywood.

below, right

The Micheltorena Street project's geometric roofline is the first hint of the shift from Mediterranean to modern in California architectural trends.

opposite

Alfresco dining with good friends during the magic hour is one of the greatest pleasures of living an indoor/outdoor lifestyle.

following pages

Lounging by the pool under the moonlight on a warm summer evening is a delightful end cap to a dinner party. Torchlight sparkles off the water and adds drama—as well as mood lighting—to the space.

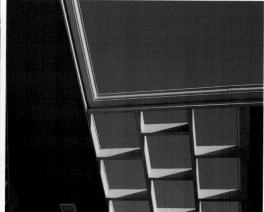

The first tier of the patio stretches out from the house itself. We treated this level, where most of the action takes place, as we would any room. We created three main areas in proportion to the patio, utilizing the available space without overcrowding the tier. We set up the dining table right in front of the French doors and framed by windows off the living room to give it a center-stage presence. To the left of the dining table, we set up a simple but elegant station to display the food before and while serving. To the right of the dining table, we created a conversation seating area with places for all eight guests to enjoy cocktails before dinner. The vintage Brown Jordan patio furniture includes a small chaise that sits three people and a few chairs surrounding two small side tables that we used as coffee tables. We also placed firm, large-sized floor pillows, covered in soft wool with a large graphic-print fabric, against the low wall behind the chaise, turning it into a kind of natural sofa. The close quarters and candlelight make the space intimate and cozy—this type of setting attracts people to it.

To dress up the main event—the dining table—we selected a vivid gold tapestry tablecloth, cut from upholstery fabric, featuring a subtly textured floral pattern in light olive green. The napkins are of a complementary tone. Arranged down the center of the table, turquoise candles in glass hurricanes added an accent color against the gold and lit up the evening. Stoneware birds and tiny bunches of yellow roses accentuate the formal place settings. Centerpieces are so important for finishing a well-dressed table and can be very simple to assemble. In addition to candles, we've placed cuttings from trees and gardens, such as dark green palm leaves, white and blue hydrangea, white and pink roses, and sea-grass papyrus, under and around serving platters. Even

decorative bowls full of colorful citrus fruits, like bright lemons and dark green limes, or glossy leaves make wonderful, quick centerpieces for impromptu entertaining.

The guests on this particular evening were a mix of people in the fashion, antiques, and interior design communities. It's always wise to invite people who share common or complementary interests. A well-planned guest list will help ensure that everyone gets along reasonably well and has an enjoyable evening. Decorating your space with unexpected pieces, such as the vintage birds on the dining table, makes for great conversation by giving guests something to comment on or react to. It also helps to have party music set and ready for different moods, whether it's swanky and classy or just ambient grooves. Some of our top go-tos are the Antonio Carlos Jobim collection, the *Best of Eartha Kitt* album, and anything by Johnny Hartman or John Coltrane. It is entertainment taboo to have guests sitting around a table in silence. Instead feel the rhythm!

below

The right guest list makes for interesting conversation, and a selection of fine and unique libations keeps the good cheer flowing.

opposite

Conversation areas should be intimate, but not crowded. These small end tables provide just enough room for drinks while allowing the surrounding chairs to cluster in close. Candles in glass hurricanes add a dash of color and ensure sufficient mood lighting as twilight draws near.

following pages

A tailor-made dining table awaits guests for an enjoyable outdoor dinner party.

Grilled Lamb Chops

arugula &

Puree Sauce

Melon Sorbet

Another nice decorative touch is incorporating handmade paper goods. Enticing the guests with a delicious menu is part of the dining experience. We made our menus with a charcoal-colored museum-board backing and two colors of paper: parchment white and celadon green. To imbue the menus with personality, the selections were handwritten. We bound everything together using green and turquoise grosgrain ribbons and velvet stylized flower accoutrements. We also found some beautiful little papers with palm/fern formations to use as place cards. We embellished the leaves and wrote the guests' names by hand. Choosing unique and personal items to dress up an event brings a special quality to the evening that is enjoyable to all; shopping for these perfect details is a fun little ritual that does the soul good.

opposite

Hand-writing your course selections gives menus a touch of personality.

below, clockwise from top left

A specially crafted invitation sent by post is a treat in the age of e-mail; add a burst of color to the table using fresh cut flowers; a handmade menu crafted with quality paper and pretty ribbons adds just the right personal touch.

following pages

Decorative birds are an element of surprise perched on a dining table in an outdoor setting, while roses add elegance and color to the temporary display. A simple way to set the stage for an outdoor party is to add splashes of color to your yard, terrace, or porch using fresh-cut flowers in vases, candles in hurricanes, oversized throw pillows, decorative rugs and throws with colorful prints, and ornate items from inside your home. This sets a festive mood, while maintaining a common visual theme flowing from the inside of your home to the outside.

above

In Southern California, evening partygoers always migrate to the backyard. Pools are like a magnet.

below

Even food can make a statement when presented with care. A Modage life is about using everyday opportunities to enjoy beauty and lushness. Unique and colorful dishes are the background; herbs, sauces, and other garnishes are the finishing decoratives.

opposite

Ron and Jaime breaking bread with friends.

On the Menu

CALIFORNIA CAPRESE
Artisan mozzarella tucked into garden tomatoes, garnished with basil, extra-virgin olive oil, and a balsamic glaze.

CARROT-GINGER SUMMER SOUP
Sunny soup with a kiss of dairy-fresh sour cream, green chives, and mango chutney.

GRILLED LAMB CHOPS
Tender, chargrilled lamb chops in a nest of crisp arugula and drizzled with herbed chimichurri sauce.

MELON SORBET
Cleansing cantaloupe, iced with sweet mint.

ROAST CHICKEN
Delicately roasted savory chicken with seasonal sweet fruits on a bed of aromatic couscous.

CREAMSICLE CORNUCOPIA
Tart kumquat granita side by side with Madagascar vanilla ice cream, nestled in a crisp pizzelle cornucopia.

SUNSET MARGARITA
Silver tequila, Cointreau, orange juice, lime juice, and sugar. Garnished with sugar–coated orange slices, mint sprigs, and a bit of sea grass.

In Los Angeles, one of our favorite ways to take in a very romantic sunset (and find inspiration) is to have an early dinner at Yamashiro in Hollywood. For nearly a century, Yamashiro has watched the progression of history. It witnessed the birth of the film industry, enjoyed the glamour of Hollywood's Golden Age, sheltered those escaping the tensions of war with Japan during World War II, and recently has enjoyed a renaissance of interest in Eastern cultures. Once a fabulous private estate, historic Yamashiro is now open to the public as a unique restaurant with accessible gardens. It sits high above famed Hollywood Boulevard—the perfect setting to enjoy an endless summer sky.

HISTORY'S MYSTERIES

Presentation is everything. Making a statement with your drinks and food, such as serving drinks in vintage tumblers with an umbrella or orchid garnish, is always a great opportunity to create a memorable experience. Invest in attractive trays or cake stands for displaying food, hors d'oeuvres, and dips. Always have a clear pitcher with a large stirrer and a cocktail shaker. Matching cloth napkins or printed paper napkins with at least eight matching wineglasses or other barware and plates is ideal, though mixing and matching is fun—as long as the pieces form a pulled-together family. Aside from vintage stores, we like to shop for unique bowls, containers, vases, and barware at specialty or boutique design stores. The finest shops should know their stuff when it comes to high-design pieces you won't want to miss. When not in use, a bar cart is a perfect place to happily display your collection of stylish pieces.

opposite

The smallest details contribute to the impact of the whole event. This gilded glass is an accessory, too.

IN GOOD TASTE

In addition to entertaining, we also design dining room installations at our store, the House of Design. Installations give us a chance to play with design ideas in exciting new ways and to show visitors and clients firsthand how pattern, scale, color, texture, and proportion can work together to create rooms that make a statement. Our inspiration for dining rooms, the hearts of all dinner parties, often comes from frequenting classic Los Angeles restaurants and experiencing fine dining the way it used to be done.

One old haunt that strikes a particular chord with us is Dresden Restaurant in Los Feliz, a ritzy old neighborhood just east of Hollywood, near Griffith Park and Observatory. The dining room, featuring decidedly Asian overtones, is a perfect time capsule of elegant Los Angeles dining enjoyment. With its dimmed lights, hints of red against dark wood, creamy white leather banquettes monogrammed with DR, brass teardrop Venetian chandeliers cascading from high ceilings, and vintage coffee carts bustling prime rib and dinner salads to tables, the Dresden envelops guests in subdued luxury. It's not the most expensive or swanky restaurant in town, but it has style—a style of its own that we love. We admire its dramatic essence, which permeates everything, and which we strive to capture in our work. The owner, Carl Ferraro, has a magical charisma and he caters to every guest with top-notch service. This seasoned establishment knows class and knows how to treat a patron, whether the early bird or the last man standing.

below, left to right

A magnificent brass chandelier hangs above the banquettes in the main dining room at the Dresden; Ron, Jaime, and restaurant owner Carl Ferraro enjoying a cocktail in the bar; classic arched canopy over the entrance.

opposite

We often take time out to enjoy afternoon tea in the dining room of our showroom. This is where our best work happens.

following pages

These wonderful decorative chandeliers over the bar of the Dresden are original to the restaurant; they add the perfect ambience for enjoying an Old Hollywood cocktail.

Pages 208-209

The Dresden, an elegant old haunt that takes us back to the golden age of Hollywood.

The successful use of contrast in such a dramatic space as the Dresden is something to be inspired by—we wanted our Exotic Craze dining room installation at the shop, influenced by a late-1930s trend, to have the same effect. Our room has a distinct Asian flair: It is done in Imperial Red, with accents of white, black, and a tiny bit of blue for a vivid color palette. The walls feature a grass-cloth textured, bamboo trellis–patterned wallpaper that picks up on the chinois bamboo-latticed chairs and matching display cabinet. The iron pagoda chandelier incorporates yet another bamboo pattern along with stylized flowers.

Over-the-top light fixtures are oh so chic, much more suited to high style than the harsh down-lights illuminating most contemporary spaces. The chandelier, ambient light fixtures, and lamps cast a theatrical glow over the space, providing enough light to see your dinner companions without losing the soft shadows that accentuate the variety of shapes in the room. The shimmery blues of the peacock feathers and chair cushions brighten things up just a little bit, enhancing the light's effect and adding texture.

And yet, among the Asian influences, the dining table itself is a heavy French-inspired piece called "Louis the Umpteenth"—made by local L.A. product designers Johnston-Ready. The table is inspired by an old form but is made with modern materials. The simple handmade black-lace tablecloth, made by clothing designer Nora Caliguri, is fashion-inspired, taking its cues from moody Parisian designs mixed with Brooklyn grit. The Savoy chairs at the head and foot of the table are made of white, faux shagreen (real shagreen is stingray hide), which feels like leather but has a slightly rough, almost scaly texture. The contrast in scale between these substantial chairs and the lighter, more open bamboo chairs adds interest. Our centerpiece, which meanders across the tabletop, is a very large candelabra molded after an actual grapevine. It is made of aluminum, an unexpectedly modern material for a room like this. For an even more surprising twist, we added faux taxidermy—tiny songbirds—on a noir, footed pie plate and under a glass cloche.

What you want to offer to your dinner guests is an experience—a place to feel special and yet relaxed. As with the Dresden, your home can be a destination: a place where people go to get away and celebrate a night out on the town. With the right mix of details, your dining room itself can be the most striking conversation piece of all.

opposite

The Red dining room at Woodson & Rummerfield's showroom harkens back to the golden age of old Hollywood and the Asian exotic craze of the 1940s.

below

Ron and Jaime in a design session with product designers Matt Ready and Stephen Johnston of Johnston-Ready; Ron and Jaime with Nora Caliguri, who creates fashion and design products inspired by fashion.

following pages

Our Imperial Red dining room installation makes a clear statement: "Glamour is here to stay!"

Living in the Moment

Why save the good stuff for special occasions? That day may never come. Our design philosophy merges with our way of living—Modage is about injecting lushness and fun into every day, enjoying your life to the fullest in any setting. Learning how to make your space a reflection of who you are and what makes you happy is the core of our work. Surrounding yourself with comfort and beauty is a great way to start making this philosophy your own. From designing grand spaces to enacting little personal rituals, if you take a bit of care, a high-style life will unfold.

WIDE-OPEN SPACES

Known as the playground to the stars, Palm Springs is a favorite weekend getaway for many Angelenos. Driving along Interstate 10 takes you away from the ocean and east into the desert hillsides. The clean desert air, sprawling mesquite trees, and the purple and sage tones of the rugged, towering peaks of the San Jacinto Mountains just take your breath away. Palm Springs is known for its natural hot springs and as a spectacular spa destination, as well as for its innovative architecture and trademark mid-century modern designs. Palm Springs also has an unwritten dress code: color, color, color, prints, prints, prints! No wonder we love it there.

Necessary items for a weekend in Palm Springs: pool, cool drink, convertible, and free time to wander about town. A great place to relax and get inspired, it is the ultimate indoor/outdoor escape. In fact, this Palm Springs home is a weekend getaway built by legendary architect Donald Wexler, best known for his innovative, out-of-this-world style and for the homes he built from the 1950s to the '70s. The desert is filled with so much open, expansive space that it allows for more avant-garde architectural design. Wexler, a former apprentice of Richard Neutra and associate of William Cody, took excellent advantage of this. In Palm Springs, Wexler designed modern homes for celebrities such as Dinah Shore, public buildings such as the Union '76 building, the Palm Springs Convention Center, and the Jetsons-like Palm Springs International Airport. In 1961, in northern Palm Springs, he built an experimental community of steel-framed homes, known as the Alexander Steel Houses. The seven Alexander homes were designed and engineered using steel for cost-effective living. Donald,

who still consults on architectural projects today, popped by for a visit and told us that each structure took only eight hours to build! The core of each structure was made of a train cargo container, with steel-framed walls on the perimeter. This allowed for innovative roofing systems and the famous zig-zag roofline—an icon of Palm Springs living—on top of clerestory glass. Perfect examples of Wexler's signature modern style, the Alexander residences are now registered historical landmarks and a hot stop on several Palm Springs tours.

previous pages, left
A toast to living in the moment while taking in a most perfect California sunset.

previous pages, right
Woodson & Rummerfield's Chrysanthemum wallpaper pattern, rendered in black-on-black.

below, left
The openness of the expansive desert around Palm Springs has inspired decades of avant-garde architectural designs, like Donald Wexler's famed Barlow House.

below, right
Ron and Jaime enjoying a walk on a warm summer's day in Palm Springs.

opposite
Succulents like this Variegated Caribbean Agave are a staple of Palm Springs landscapes.

following pages
The zigzag roofline of the Barlow House is a signature Palm Springs design icon.

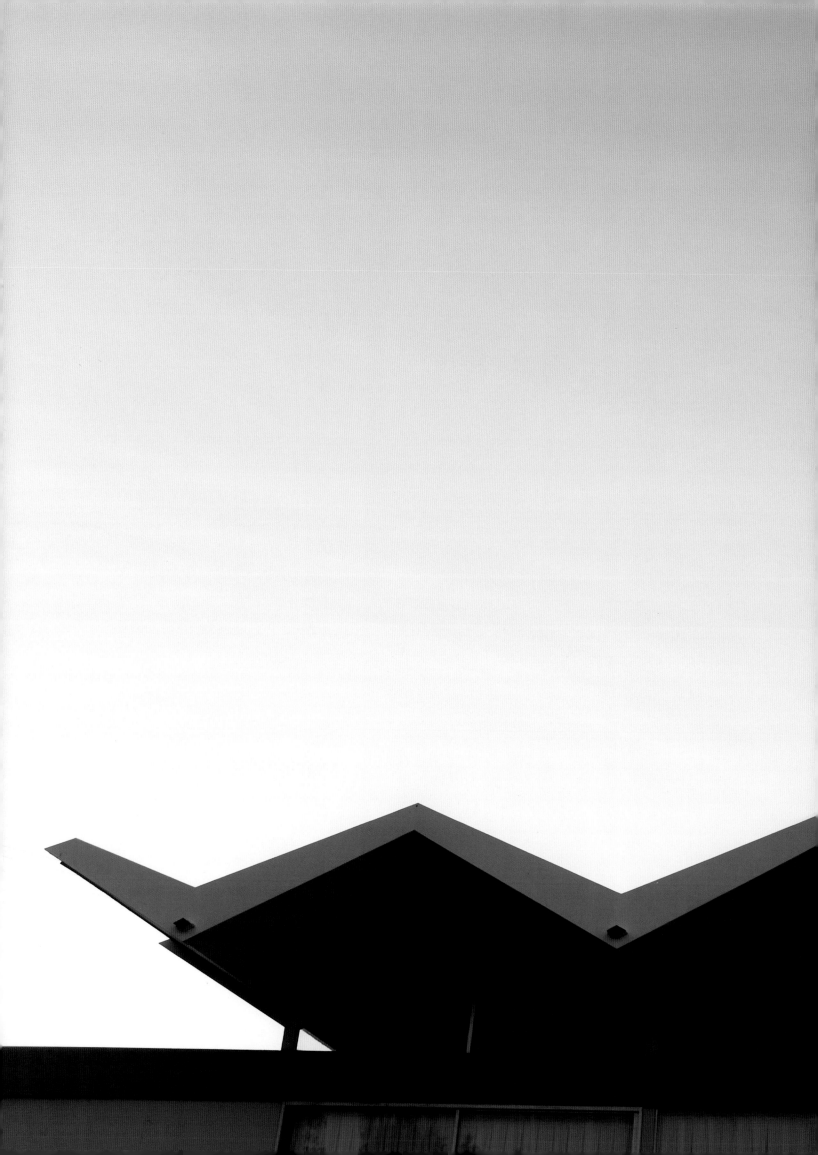

The Barlow House is an Alexander that had been completely renovated and restored to its original design by the previous owners. It is a fantastic mid-century modern home, the kind of pedigreed architecture that so captures the essence of Palm Springs. It has a very contemporary, forward look that is, somehow, still illustrative of the desert's glory days of the 1950s and '60s. Like the rest of Palm Springs, the Barlow House is timeless and instantly recognizable.

When entering the house, a sense of calm comes over you. Our clients wanted the interior design to stay true to the house's heritage, so we used a lot of clean lines, crisp architectural lighting, and white-on-white furniture. We softened the effect of floor-to-ceiling glass windows with flowing cotton drapery, also in white, that sways in the desert breeze and provides tantalizing glimpses of the sparkling pool beyond. The house is very minimal, uncluttered but not stark—there's so much to tempt the eye. A lot of people strive for this kind of streamlined luxury in their homes, but are endlessly frustrated because they have too much stuff for living their daily lives. Since the Barlow House is a vacation home, it's easier to keep the interior sparse and airy. It's important for a vacation home to make space for relaxation and enjoyment of the moment instead of providing yet more everyday distractions, particularly in Palm Springs, where unattached breeziness is a lifestyle. People come here to relax, unwind, and enjoy a simpler way of life.

In keeping with the high style of the architecture, we outfitted the Barlow House with only high-design pieces by respected names such as Florence Knoll, Philippe Starck, and Fritz Hansen. To keep the look from becoming too serious, we added whimsical, true-to-era accessories, such as colored-glass vases clustered on a marble coffee table and mercury glass pieces, throughout the home; these pieces also provide punches of color and shine. These types of decorative objects keep the design authentic and are a staple of any Palm Springs modern house. A fluffy white shag rug anchors the Carrara marble coffee table in the living room and adds a tactile surprise to the otherwise smooth finish of the concrete floor.

Homes in Palm Springs are often a bit different from their owners' homes in Los Angeles. That's what makes these houses true destinations: out-of-the-ordinary experiences that remove you from daily routines and give you room to fully enjoy living in the moment.

below
Jaime enjoying the desert sunset from the Wexler living room.

opposite
Mercury glass decoratives in a variety of shapes and sizes add shine to a room.

following pages
Floor-to-ceiling windows draped with cotton curtains take full advantage of the bright desert sun without letting it get too harsh. The room's white-on-white color palette helps keep things light and airy, while unexpected clusters of vintage collectibles provide splashes of colorful fun. Low furniture with clean lines and tall pieces of art celebrate the zigzag roofline instead of taking attention from it.

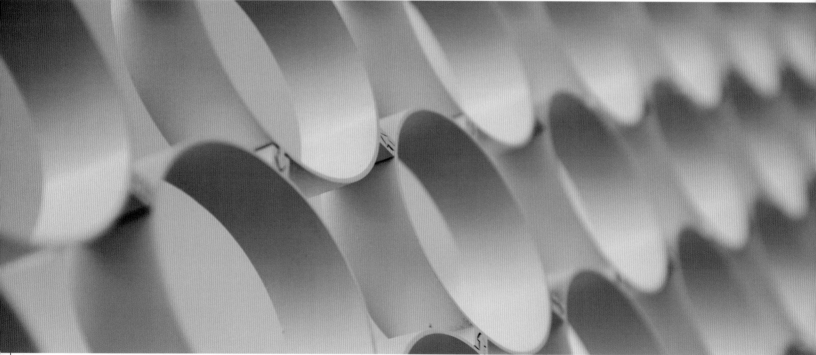

above

An array of like-colored decoratives adds impact to a room without disturbing the tranquil, monochromatic palette, while just a few carefully placed colored pieces keep it from feeling stark. A geometric-patterned room divider, also in white, adds a modern twist and visual impact.

opposite

A most comforting sitting room at the Barlow House.

following pages

No home in Palm Springs is complete without a sparkling swimming pool.

Julius Shulman: A Day in the Life

One day, it was brought to our attention that Julius Shulman wanted to photograph the Barlow House. Shulman has photographed over seven decades worth of astounding indoor/outdoor architectural works by designers such as Charles Eames, Eero Saarinen, Craig Ellwood, Pierre Koenig, Richard Neutra, and William Wurster, for John Entenza's *Arts & Architecture* magazine and the Case Study Houses program, among other projects. Shulman's work has followed the pioneers of American modern design, especially those who brought new thinking, techniques, and materials to post-war California house building. But in his 70-year career, he hadn't had the opportunity to photograph much, if any, of Donald Wexler's work on private residences. He had selected a handful of Wexler's homes to photograph, and our project was one of them.

Shulman—spry as ever at age 94—and his crew drove up in a Volkswagen van to have a look at his muse. It was so incredible to meet Julius (who was partial to Buddy, our design dog); he photographed with the most skilled eye, still sharp and precise as ever. The Polaroids alone captured the magic and architectural wonder of the home in a way we had never seen on film. We still wonder how he did it. Luckily, the photos he took of the Barlow House will be on exhibition in the Palm Springs Art Museum, a modernist institution, for all to see.

top
Julius Shulman taking a moment to enjoy Buddy's company.

bottom
Jaime and Julius take a look at test shots of the Barlow House.

opposite
Jaime, Julius, and his crew working to capture a masterful shot.

HAPPY HABITAT

One of the things that makes us happy is the affection of our pets, who are truly funny characters. We're animal lovers. It's not uncommon to see us at a swanky function with one of our dogs as an escort. They bring us so much joy, laughter, and companionship. It's no surprise to our clients that our dogs are spoiled rotten and considered a member of our team and family. Their actions tell us they love design, too: Buddy covers his eyes with his paws when he sees south-western patterns; Niles plays dead if someone passes by with carnations or baby's breath in a flower arrangement; and Petra barks profusely when the lighting is too bright.

Because animals and animal rights are so important to us, we were thrilled to be given the opportunity to design the Los Angeles offices of the People for the Ethical Treatment of Animals (PETA). Designing for PETA is a great example of finding a way to let what's close to your heart shine through in your surroundings. Designs that truly reflect the inhabitants' personalities and interests have authenticity, a feeling of being home, that cannot be imitated.

As you can imagine, to design for PETA meant we could not use materials that in any way harmed an animal. For example, we couldn't use silk because silk manufacturing damages the ecosystem and homes of the silkworm; wool was out because sheep are shorn in a way that PETA considers inhumane. This posed quite a challenge for us. But we quickly understood the reasoning behind these restrictions, and by the end of the project, we were very well-versed in the use of synthetic and other alternative products. It was exciting to learn new ways to let our designs reflect what's important to our clients and us.

The result was fantastic and as animal-friendly as you can get. We used volumes of man-made, animal-free products, such as vinyl furniture coverings instead of leather. All the wall art was created with vegetable dye and hung in frames made from reclaimed wood. The wide-open room called for curtain partitions, which are all cotton and polyester. Bright shades of orange and plum bring some energy to the work space, while earthy, olive green accents warm up the somewhat industrial setting. A fun circle pattern on the sofa contrasts nicely with the square pattern of the rug. The large painted stripes of the wall create a fantastic play on scale against the smaller rectangles of the brick wall. The offices turned out impressively, and the PETA staff was ecstatic. They loved our work so much that they asked us to lend our design talent to their 25th-anniversary party, held on the back lots of Paramount Pictures studios. The party-cum-fundraiser was a star-studded affair, hosted by Pamela Anderson and Alec Baldwin. It was very moving to see so many people turn out to support such a worthy cause.

opposite
Jaime and Ron with high-style furry friends Buddy and Niles.

below, left
Buddy examining fabric samples for Woodson and Rummerfield's clients; PETA's new chic offices.

below, right
A sitting area in PETA's new animal-friendly offices.

following pages
In our hands, PETA's L.A. office became a colorful workspace made up of materials that did not harm or disturb any animal habitats.

231

EXIT

DOWN TO EARTH

Keeping our world beautiful is also very important to us. We believe that eco-friendly design can be cool without being crunchy, and we often incorporate natural and sustainable products into our work.

For example, our clients' home on Nolden Street is an eco-friendly house built in 1965 by Los Angeles architect James Allen Walters. Nolden Street is nestled in the hillside right between Hollywood and Pasadena in an area called Saint Francis Heights, one of the oldest neighborhoods in Los Angeles. The house features a unique, cut diamond–shaped footprint: The front is wide, with the house narrowing toward the back until it comes to a culet-like point. In wonderful contrast to its innovative shape, the house was built using a classic 1960s post-and-beam approach. With a very organic palette and a surrounding landscape of indigenous succulents and potted plants, this is a naturally happy house.

The structure of the house is made of cedar wood, while the interior features a lot of walnut, including walnut cabinets. The rear of the house, which faces west, is constructed of eighteen-foot walls of glass and wood; this allows the Southern California sunshine to permeate the house, minimizing the need for artificial lighting and heat during the day. The furniture is all 1950s-'70s vintage, such as an original Herman Miller Noguchi table, patterned rugs from Tibet and Mexico, authentic Le Klint and Nelson bubble lamps, and a massive three-piece sectional sofa in its original woven textile. We believe using vintage is an excellent way to recycle—after all, it is adaptive reuse. In this house, the only updating was to replace older appliances with more modern, energy-efficient versions.

below
A bounty of succulents adorns the yard at our Nolden Street project.

opposite
In our Nolden Street project, we kept the natural, organic feel of the house by keeping its original materials as much as possible, such as these beautiful wood panels. The home is outfitted with vintage furniture and art: Using antique pieces is a great example of adaptive reuse that is in keeping with high-style design.

following pages
Party guests enjoying each other's company and the California sunset.

opposite

The kitchen and dining room at our Nolden Street project has an open floor plan that echoes the openness of the window-walls and makes entertaining easy.

above, clockwise from top left

Carolyn and Patrick working magic in the kitchen for the party-goers, who enjoy this perfect summer buffet; Marisa looks strikingly similar to a Jonathan Adler pillow; mixing and matching tabletop ware makes for an exciting table.

following pages

A magical view of the rear of Woodson and Rummerfield's Nolden Street project architectural post and beam.

above, clockwise from top left

Unique vintage collections fill the sunny home, reminding us of days gone by; a mix of new and old-school items add nostalgia and bring out the owner's personality; vintage decorative pottery surrounds the Numark DJ turntable; the party gets rockin' when the vinyl records come out.

opposite

This sun-filled living room features original pieces such as Isamu Noguchi coffee table, woven Jonathan Adler pillows, and a mint-condition 1970s sectional sofa with its original fabric intact. High-hanging light fixtures provide evening illumination without interfering with the conversation or the view. A soft, shaggy rug grounds the expansive space and keeps things cozy.

THE ENVIRONMENT

There are so many simple things you can do to live in a more environmentally friendly way. We like to "think globally and act locally." For instance, use eco-friendly paints: Ask your retailer about low or zero VOC (volatile organic compounds) formulations. Install low-flow showerheads and low-flush toilets. Try a homegrown centerpiece for the dining table instead of cut flowers, and make landscape choices that are in tune with your natural environment. Adding dimmer switches and keeping lights dim as much as possible utilizes less electricity and lends ambience to a room—replacing regular lightbulbs with energy-efficient bulbs saves you money, too. Tung oil works great as a natural wood finish, and there are many beautiful accents available for your home made from natural or recycled material, such as crushed glass or stone tiles and organic cotton and linen textiles. And whenever possible, maximize the natural flow of air in your home by designing in lots of insulated windows—this allows you to use the air-conditioning a lot less and saves energy.

opposite

A tranquil, woodsy view helps make any home feel more peaceful. Use lots of well-insulated windows to take advantage of the scenery—and the sunlight—as much as possible.

top

A vintage 1960s light fixture adorns the side of a mid-century home.

bottom

Outside, indigenous California succulents are a naturally beautiful landscape addition.

LUSH LIFE

Taking in nature is nurturing to the soul. There's nothing like sitting outdoors and breathing the fresh air. Just taking a moment to sit and breathe can slow down the overactive whir of your mind and life. It's okay to stop and gaze at the ocean, watch the leaves fall, and smell the magnolias.

Take some time to visit your local parks and beaches and enjoy the accessible beauty waiting for you there. Imagine taking your fine china, stemware, friends, family, and pets to a natural space for a lovely afternoon picnic. How divine! That china is not doing you any good sitting in the cabinet, so why not use it? We do it all the time and meet the most interesting people in the process, all without a single china or crystal casualty. We also love to bring decorative pillows, candlesticks and candelabras, and fresh-cut flowers in a vase to dress things up. Our ideal picnic menu includes delicious gourmet foods and champagne; as with any type of enter-

taining, decorative trays, serving pieces, and pitchers perk up your spread. For more interesting and comfortable seating options, we leave the lawn chairs at home and cart along sweet little ottomans, light side chairs, and oversized pillows for lounging under the open sky.

opposite
We frequently take time to enjoy the beauty of natural surroundings by spending a day in the park.

Every picnic requires a picnic blanket. We love to bring a selection of soft, luxurious textile remnants to arrange on the ground. Much better than a ratty old blanket, a beautiful piece of fabric serves as a backdrop for your perfect outdoor afternoon and takes your picnic from casual to casually elegant.

JEWELRY FOR THE HOME

AFTERWORD

Your life is the special occasion, so celebrate it every chance you get! We believe in creating fabulously memorable experiences. Opportunities to indulge and enjoy come to all of us every day—we believe in seizing the moment to create a memory, because there is no guarantee of tomorrow.

Our hope is that we've provided some inspiration for you to inject a little high style into your world and set the stage for a truly luscious life. Great design creates the backdrop, but it's how you live every day that counts. Indulge in the little rituals that make you happy, whether it's sipping a morning cappuccino out of an antique teacup, writing letters on hand-engraved stationery using your favorite pen, sleeping under a vintage quilt, using the good silver, or splurging on fresh flowers every week. Whatever suits your fancy, if it makes your soul sing, even for a few minutes each day, it matters.

When it comes down to it, we believe in the importance of taking note of and creating beauty around ourselves— and acknowledging the things and experiences that bring us joy. We could all use a little more joy.

opposite
Enjoy your most prized possessions, why hide them away? Use the silver everyday.

below
Take time to do the things that make you happy. Hand-write a letter on sumptuous paper. Indulge by surrounding yourself with fragrant and gorgeous flowers weekly. Enjoy your cappuccino in an old, beautiful cup.

following pages
Our muse: a sweeping view of Los Angeles at night.

Acknowledgments

Thanks to Jonathan Shapiro for dedicating your talent and time to making our vision a reality through your photography.

Also, to Skye Moorhead, Karyn Millet, and Brad Benson, for your photographic talents.

Thanks to Ally Peltier, our writer, who turned our thought processes into text worthy of the company of these gorgeous images.

Thanks to Jon Ritt and his staff, Anthony Jagoda, and Brian Toth for their incredible graphic design capabilities to tell our story visually and magically.

We also want to thank all of the people who assisted us in the success of this book. We are constantly inspired by you and thank you for all of your contributions and support:

Julius Shulman
Harry Lederman and Sandy Gooch Lederman
Beverly and Larry Schnur
Trina Turk
Mattia Biagi
Roberto Cavalli
Carolyn Baker
Dana Rummerfield
Tom Stanley
Patrick Ediger
Sarah Aronson
Jadrian Johnson
Lauren Bragg
Patricia Cantor
Sara Ruffin Costello
Lawrence Daniels Esq.
Anthony Keats Esq.
Jonathan Adler
Alan Rohwer
Jayne Heagney
Jen Dolan
Jamie Drake
Mark Mayfield
Brad Benson
Walter Castro
Michael Gruber
Ken Hilgendorf Construction
Surena Fisch
Andy Cohen
Mark Freeman Esq.
CPSphere
Frank Weimann, The Literary Group
Mark Armfield Construction

Vanessa Veloso
Henry Sahakin (Melrose Carpets)
Hector Gomez
Wayne Fenske and Chad Khun
David Hrowbowski, The Cufflink King
Allen Baran Paint and Wallpaper
Wyatt Sweitzer and the crew at Back Breakers
Amos Feldman
Efren Eguren
Charmaine Barnes
Jenny Lapat
Laurie Rubenstein
Megan Luchini
David Lefkowitz
Doug Gelvin
Carl Ferarro
Dave Casey
Rollence Patagun
Aaron Kirsch
Matt Johnston
Stephen Ready
Sami Hayek
Stefan Lawrence
Ceasar and Jonathan Tajada
Richard Rubio and Isaias Gonzales
Kris K. Quinn
Bobby Trendy
Sera Hersham, Sera of London
Brendan Vaughan
Reggie Cheong-Lee and Peter Spieglhagen
Ceasar Basurto
David and Helen Lennie
Tracee and Mike Falkow
Amelie Escher
Bradley Smith, Roberto Cavalli
Chase Ferguson
John Connell and John Hall
Philip Stites, Therien & Co.
Michael Sipling
Selma and Suad Cisic
Vanessa De Vargas
Donald Wexler

Our clients, who welcome design integration at its finest: Kendall and Matthew Rhodes; Jonathan Anastas; Suzanne Marques and Robert Dourisboure; Christina Aguilera and Jordan Bratman; Kelly Preston and John Travolta; Courtney Love; Eric and Carmel Greenberg; the Ritt family; Douglas Harris; Chris Weiss and Lisa Buch; Richard and Patricia Cantor; Marilyn Rummerfield and Dick Seay; PETA;

Esquire magazine; and Versace.

Domino magazine

House Beautiful magazine

Western Interiors magazine

Angeleno magazine

Space magazine

Metropolitan Home magazine

Jaime's family, especially Dana, Mom, Dad, Sam, Christopher, Jackie, Amanda, Grandma Baker, Grandma Celia, and Grandpa "Sam."

Jaime's close friends, Elena Frampton, Tracee Falkow, Stacy Smith, Jon Ritt, Carson Johns, Ane Rocha, Alan Robles, Gina Kida, Stacy Keanan, Guy Birtwhistle, Marisa and Ryan Dupuis, Thomas Krauss, Suzanne Marques, and Shay Watson.

The people who kept me looking good: Robyn and Michelle at Wax Poetic and Byron and Paul at Byron Williams Salon.

Ron's family, especially Mom, Julie, Tom, Raquel, Shirley, Kathie, and Aunt Gen (My Auntie Mame).

Ron's close friends, Jim Bibb, Carolyn and Will Hobbs, Darrell Ingram, Peter Obermayer, Gerardo Peron, Tim Scowden, Steven Perry, Ron Orr, Richard Bernstein, Vanni Vezzosi, Herb Johnson, Jim Downey, Wayne Fenske, Jeff Frank, Michael Martinez, Michael Gilbeaux, Mark Suber, Mark Brand, Lawrence Lichter, Floyd Prewitt, Karen Marcus, Rashawn Levias, Regina Jones, Anthony Calderon, Bernard Boudreaux, Jack Miller, Charles Champion, Harry Clay, Ray Davi, Damaris Rosado, and Arturo Molina.

To the memory of those who inspire us: Buddy Woodson, Bobby Short, Roger Hall, Salvatore Laurella, Mary Louise Baker, Patty Baker, John Berg, Paul Williams, Richard Neutra, Elsie de Wolfe, and Billy Haines.

Beverly and Larry Schnur residence, pages 124-125: Interior Design by Neil Korpinen and Rick Erickson of Korpinen-Erickson Inc., 1187 Coast Village Road #537, Santa Barbara, CA 93108, 805-884-0019, neil@k-e-inc.com; Landscape Design by Joseph Marek of Joseph Marek Landscape Architecture, 2252 25th St., Santa Monica, CA 90405, 310-399-7923

Our team at Chronicle Books. Thank you for this magical opportunity.

Our clients who patronize our showroom. You make Los Angeles shine!

Jaime's mentors: John McCulley, Tom Witt, and Beverly Brandt at Arizona State University.

Ron's mentors: Vernon Applegate, Gioi Tran, Anya Larkin, and Martha Angus.

Thank you.

RESOURCES

Decorating Editors of McCall's. *McCall's Decorating Book.* New York: Random House. 1964.

de Wolf, Elsie. *House in Good Taste.* New York: Rizzoli, 2004.

Hale, Jonathan. *Old Way of Seeing: How Architecture Lost its Magic - And How to Get it Back.* Boston: Houghton Miffin Company, 1995.

Hudson, Karen E. *Paul R. Williams, Architect: A Legacy of Style.* New York: Rizzoli, 1993.

Goodwin, Betty. *Chasen's: Where Hollywood Dined.* Santa Monica: Angel City Press, 1996.

Gossel, Peter. *Julius Shulman: Architecture and Its Photography.* Cologne, Germany: Taschen America LLC, 1998.

Lamprecht, Barbara. *Neutra: The Complete Work.* Cologne, Germany: Tashcen America LLC, 2000.

O'Neill, Helen. *Florence Broadhurst: Her Secret & Extraordinary Lives.* San Francisco: Chronicle Books LLC, 2007.

ADDITIONAL CREDITS

Page 47, bottom: Skye Moorhead

Page 50, top: A vintage room rendering by Helen Edel Sloan from 1962 .

Page 128, bottom: Skye Moorhead

The Art Archive/ Culver City Pictures, p. 56 Florence Broadhurst, pp. 33, 38, 61, 94 (right, custom color by Woodson & Rummerfield's), 145, 183, 215 The Bruce Torrence Hollywood Photograph Collection, pp. 88, 137, 202 Domino Magazine, p. 6 Patrick Ediger, p. 22 (bottom right) Foster, p. 230 Kobal Collection, p. 122 Karyn Millet, pp. 35, 170, 171, 174, 178, 179 (top), 180, 181, 248, 249 (left) Skye Moorhead, pp. 18, 47 (bottom), 52, 54, 55, 58 (top left, top right), 74, 120, 128, 130, 131, 132, 133, 134, 135, 136, 147, 157, 162, 163, 165, 185, 221, 224 (top right), 225, 231 (right), 232, 233 Jonny Ritt, p. 49 Dana Rummerfield, pp. 58 (bottom row), 59 (left) Jaime Rummerfield, pp. 26, 27, 121 Jon Shapiro, p. 113 Helen Edel Sloan, p. 50 (top) Tom Stanley, pp. 59 (middle and right), 155 (bottom), 211 (right) Elsie de Wolfe, p. 56 Ron Woodson, pp. 24, 25 Woodson & Rummerfield's, p. 123

INDEX

A

Adler, Jonathan, 17, 237

Alexander Steel Houses, 213, 217

Alfawir, Guglielmo, 152, 153

Allen, Robert, 88, 91

Alva, Tony, 75

Anastas, Jonathan, 64, 65, 72, 75, 78, 84

Animals, ceramic, 170

ARCO Center, 72

Asian figurines and artwork, 172

B

Barlow House, 213, 217, 221, 225

Baughman, Milo, 153, 158

Bauhaus, 65, 72

Bayer, Herbert, 72

Belle Époque, 34

Bertoia, Harry, 153

Beverly Hills, 105

Biagi, Mattia, 50, 75

Bonnet, Ted, 64

Bonnet House, 64–65, 69, 72, 75, 84

Briard, Georges, 29

Broadhurst, Florence, 6, 88, 91, 95, 99, 148

Burton, Tim, 95

C

Caliguri, Nora, 208

Candles, 197

Case Study Houses program, 225

Chasen estate, 125

Chrome Heart, 75

Ciro's, 134

Cody, William, 213

Color, 38

Connell, John, 148

Corbusier, Le, 43, 44

Crawford, Joan, 130

D

Da Vinci, Leonardo, 43

Davis, Sammy, Jr., 19

Design

    eco-friendly, 229, 240

    elements of, 29, 34–35, 38, 41, 44

process of, 48, 50

Dining rooms, 201, 208

Dourisboure, Robert, 85, 88, 95

Dresden Room, 201, 208

Duke, Doris, 19

E

Eames, Charles, 153, 225

Eco-friendly design, 229, 240

Elkins, Frances, 175

Ellington, Duke, 19

Ellwood, Craig, 225

Entenza, John, 225

Entertaining, 185, 189, 194, 197–99

Esquire magazine showcase house, 56, 130, 133

F

Ferraro, Carl, 201

Ford, Tom, 65

Furniture

    accessorizing, 152

    refinishing and reupholstering, 148

    shopping for, 144

G

Gardner, Emma, 105

Gibbings, John, 72

Gobo, George, 29

Golden Ratio, 43, 44

Goodall, Edward, 29

Gropius, Walter, 65

Gucci, 75

Guns N' Roses, 134

H

Haines, Billy, 75

Halston, 88

Hansen, Fritz, 217

Hayek, Sami, 17

Hermès, 75

Hollywood, 64, 121, 125, 133

Hollywood Regency style, 125

Houdini, Harry, 85

I

IGE, 166, 175

J

Jacobsen, Arne, 72

John, Elton, 134

Johnston, Stephen, 208

Johnston-Ready, 208

K

Kennedy, Robert Woods, 65

Knoll, Florence, 95, 217

Koenig, Pierre, 225

L

LaChapelle, David, 95, 99

Lamprecht, Barbara, 64

Laurel Canyon, 85

Leibovitz, Annie, 95

Le Klint, 229, 237

Lennie, David, 17

Lighting, 53, 208

Loewy, Raymond, 161

Los Angeles

    influence of, 9, 57

    neighborhoods in, 59

Love, Courtney, 105, 109, 118

Lynch, David, 95

M

Majorelle, 105, 118

Marques, Suzanne, 85, 88, 95

McCobb, Paul, 65

Mensware showroom installation, 161, 166

Mies van der Rohe, 72

Miller, Herman, 229

Mix, Tom, 85

Modage

    definition of, 6

    inspiration for, 125

    origins of, 9

    philosophy of, 211

Mood boards, 48

Moooi, 95, 161

Moreno, Antonio, 185

N

Nelson, George, 229, 237

Neutra, Richard, 64, 65, 69, 72, 84, 213, 225

Newson, Marc, 166

Noguchi, Isamu, 229, 237

Nolden Street project, 229, 236–37

P

Palm Springs, 213, 217

Panton, Verner, 69, 72

Paramount Pictures, 228

Pattern, 34

PETA (People for the Ethical Treatment of Animals), 228

Picnics, 242–43

Poulsen, Louis, 72

Prelle Fabric Mill, 105, 109, 118

Preston, Kelly, 138–40

Proportion, 44, 53

R

Ready, Matt, 208

Rhodes, Kendall, 166, 170, 172, 175

Robs-John Gibbings, T. H., 75

Rohwer, Alan, 56, 133

S

Saarinen, Eero, 99, 225

Sacks, Ann, 139

Saint Francis Heights, 229

Santa Monica, 166

Scale, 35

Schnur, Beverly and Larry, 125

Schultz, Richard, 125

Sera of London, 118

Shopping tips, 144

Shore, Dinah, 213

Shulman, Julius, 225

Silver Lake Hills, 185

Smith, Paul, 91

Spence, Edmond, 72

Springer, Karl, 69, 72, 75, 88

Starck, Philippe, 78, 217

Stites, Philip, 22

Sue et Mar, 105, 118

T

Texture, 41

Tiffany, 95, 99

Travolta, John, 138

V

Versace, 17, 56, 130, 133–34

Versace, Donatella, 133, 134

Versace, Gianni, 133, 134

Vitruvius, 43

W

Walk of Style, 133–34

Walters, James Allen, 229

Walters, Steven, 153

Wanders, Marcel, 95

Wexler, Donald, 213, 225

Wiinblad, Bjørn, 148

Williams, Paul, 125

Woodson & Rummerfield's House of Design

    design of, 13

    location of, 13

    opening of, 13

    origins of, 19

Wurster, William, 225

Y

Yamashiro, 199